The Open University

Book 1

Lives of Objects

Edited by Susie West and Katy Soar

This publication forms part of the Open University module A105 *Voices, texts and material culture*. Details of this and other Open University modules can be obtained from the Student Registration and Enquiry Service, The Open University, PO Box 197, Milton Keynes MK7 6BJ, United Kingdom (tel. +44 (0)845 300 60 90; email general-enquiries@open.ac.uk).

Alternatively, you may visit the Open University website at www.open.ac.uk where you can learn more about the wide range of modules and packs offered at all levels by The Open University.

To purchase a selection of Open University materials visit www.ouw.co.uk, or contact Open University Worldwide, Walton Hall, Milton Keynes MK7 6AA, United Kingdom for a catalogue (tel. +44 (0)1908 858779; fax +44 (0)1908 858787; email ouw-customer-services@open.ac.uk).

The Open University, Walton Hall, Milton Keynes MK7 6AA

First published 2014

Edited and designed by The Open University.

Typeset by The Open University.

Printed and bound in the United Kingdom by Halstan Printing Group, Amersham.

ISBN 978 1 7800 7820 5

1.1

Contents

Introduction

Somewhere in fourteenth-century Italy, the author Francesco Petrarch (1304–1374) was sitting in his study reading about the Roman emperors. He paused from his reading to make a note in the margin of the book, because he had realised that the statement he had just read could be contradicted. The author's claim that a particular emperor had been handsome did not match Petrarch's impression of a portrait of the same emperor on a coin. So he jotted down his own conclusion, thinking it likely that the image on the coin, issued during the emperor's reign, was more honest than the flattering author. In other words, Petrarch paid different types of sources equal attention and realised that they disagreed (Haskell, 1995, p. 1). He thought about their different contexts – one description was produced during the time of the emperor; the other used a standard way of writing about imperial leaders – to help him make a judgement.

The chapters in this book take up Petrarch's problem of how to use and make sense of an object as part of the process of answering questions. Petrarch's coin was already centuries old when he looked at it. It wasn't in use as currency but it did still have a use: as a visual source for a historical issue. It was a familiar object, similar in design and function to the coins Petrarch used daily. However, many other objects that survive from the past may no longer be familiar to us, perhaps because their design has changed radically over time, or because their original functions were specific to the needs of the people who made them. Objects that made sense to their original owners may no longer be easily understood by later generations or by people from other cultures. Objects that do not make sense are at risk of being ignored, or discarded, or misinterpreted. Many objects survive as historical artefacts on display in museums, but apart from looking beautiful, valuable or curious, it may not be obvious to most visitors what they once meant or why they are still interesting.

Objects created by humans are defined as cultural, and take their place within the broad set of human activities that contribute towards the relations of humans with each other and with their social worlds. Objects are the physical expression of ideas that humans have developed to explain the world around them and to manage the challenges of existence. In studying objects, then, we study ourselves, as a species, and the diversity of human experience through time and across the planet.

The challenges relating to how we develop and use methods for working with objects in the humanities in order to understand their creation and meanings have been tackled by the disciplines that are introduced in these chapters. Across the book you will work with concepts and methods from Anthropology, Archaeology and Art History. These ways of working with objects in the humanities are widely used by these disciplines. In addition, in Chapters 1 and 2 you will find material showing how these approaches can work within Music, while the final chapter tackles a field of learning that unites the study of texts and the study of objects by looking at the book as an object. Before thinking about what these shared concepts and methods are, however, I shall introduce the three key disciplines involved: Anthropology, Archaeology and Art History.

Academic interest in cultural objects is organised through these disciplines, which prioritise the physical, material evidence of human activity. The first, Anthropology, is the study of humans across different cultures (both past and living), in order to compare and understand the variety of ways in which humans organise their societies and use culture. The second discipline, Archaeology, involving the study of the material human past, has been particularly concerned to solve the challenges of objects that come to us without written explanations or living practitioners of surviving traditions. Finally, Art History works with the visual culture of societies and related textual sources, past and present, to investigate the production, uses and meaning of works of art.

Defining in one sentence a discipline that has emerged over centuries of scholarly effort presents a challenge. If you have previously studied AA100 *The arts past and present*, you will understand from your work there on Benin that the study of Anthropology emerged during the major phase of colonial expansion by western nations and can be linked to the imposition of colonial rule and the looting of cultural objects. In recent decades, Archaeology has borrowed many approaches from Anthropology using methods developed to investigate living societies to study past societies. Art History continues to produce debates about how to define an artwork (which might be of equal interest to both an anthropologist and an archaeologist), and to acknowledge that the definitions are heavily interlinked with the international art market. Chapter 1 discusses the historical development of Archaeology and Anthropology and their methods and concepts, to give you the background to how they have shaped the study of material culture today.

These three disciplines, which come together in Material Culture Studies, all have in common the need to display objects. Objects that have been collected together in order to be studied and to educate audiences have a long tradition of being displayed in museums in the western world. Many specialists in the three disciplines work as curators of museum collections and conduct research on these collections. For museum visitors, this is where the methods for analysing and understanding objects are most visible: the objects are selected and brought together in particular ways, depending on what the curator wishes to demonstrate.

Chapter 1 looks at selected historical examples of museum displays to discuss how the ways in which objects are brought together influences how they are interpreted. Most museums regularly update their displays, as scholarly knowledge and understanding change, and as ways of interpreting collections for visitors develop. But one survivor from the nineteenth century has not changed its displays, which now have their own historical interest; this is the Pitt Rivers Museum, part of the University of Oxford. Chapter 2 continues the theme of how objects are displayed, by looking in detail at how objects can be described and classified, and what the consequences of different ways of classifying objects might be.

Displaying objects together is one example of how objects have contexts: the glass case, the other objects selected for display, the wider purpose of the museum – all these are contexts that influence our approach to an object. Contexts, broadly defined as the relationships between things, words and ideas, help narrow down which meanings are relevant: we use contexts every day to decide, for example, which clothes to wear (are you going to work, or to the beach?), or whether to make a joke about a sad situation (will your sad friend appreciate the humour?). Context supports the meaning that is relevant in those circumstances: an object in a museum glass case has meanings associated with being selected, conserved and interpreted that it may never have had before. If you have studied AA100 *The arts past and present*, you will have encountered discussions of events and personalities that make use of a range of contexts (political, social and historical) in order to draw out why something is meaningful, then and now. The study of objects looks at the relationships between associated objects and social practices, events and people, to reach conclusions about the meaning and significance of objects. Chapter 3 investigates how contexts (things, words and ideas) that are associated with the objects of study can be used, particularly by anthropologists in living societies and by archaeologists working on the past society of Pompeii in Italy. Contexts for objects change as the object moves from one stage of its life to another, as Petrarch's Roman coin moved from being currency in the Roman empire to being kept in the author's medieval house as a historical object.

The final approach that is used across this book is the idea that objects have life stories, or biographies, that can be told and which can be used to show how meaning changes over a lifetime. Objects acquire meaning through their interaction with the people who produce and use them. Like people, objects have social lives which might extend over many generations of human owners. An object biography traces the life of an object from production, through use, and into an 'afterlife' as it passes out of ordinary use and becomes a museum object (Petrarch's Roman coin entered his personal collection). The model of a biography is valuable when looking closely at the history of a single object, as art historians tend to do, or when following a group of related objects, as archaeologists and anthropologists may do. These ways of working with material culture, using the model of object biographies, and researching contexts and classification at different stages of the object's life, are brought together in Chapter 4, which looks at how printed books were created and used during a historical period, *c.*1450–1800. This chapter follows the circumstances of making and using an early modern book, and shows how the material text became a bearer of meanings well beyond the words it contained. It also considers the afterlife of surviving historic books, which may now be valuable in art market terms or historically significant because of a previous owner. All of the approaches developed by Anthropology, Archaeology and Art History can be used on an object that is not usually the focus of any of these three disciplines, and the chapter invites you to stop taking for granted such a useful object as the book (even if you like to read digital texts).

The humanities are made up of academic disciplines: seven are covered in AA100 *The arts past and present*. Archaeology, Anthropology and Art History have contributed to the methods, approaches and case studies in this book. However, as you read through the chapters it will be steadily apparent that there are no strong walls between these disciplines. They all have in common the practice of writing, as an essential method for developing and sharing research. Chapter 4 takes further the idea that the material form of what is written and printed also shapes how the word is interpreted and received. As you read on through the module and turn towards the analysis of texts, I hope you will continue to reflect on how the physical properties of your study materials influence your experience and become part of your material world.

Reference

Haskell, F. (1995) *History and its Images: Art and the Interpretation of the Past*, New Haven, CN, and London, Yale University Press.

Chapter 1
What is material culture?

Rodney Harrison with Fiona Richards

Contents

Aims

This chapter will:

- introduce you to the study of material culture
- develop your knowledge and understanding of the origin of material culture as an area of study in late nineteenth- and early twentieth-century archaeology and anthropology museums
- introduce you to the concepts of 'object biography' and the 'life cycles' of things
- show how objects help to define and shape people and societies.

Materials you will need

In this chapter, you will need to watch the following film, which can be found on the module website:

- Malinowski and the Kula cycle.

You will also need to listen to the following audio recording, which can be found on the module website:

- Joshua Bell playing Massenet.

You will also be directed to the website for an online activity.

Introduction

This chapter introduces an important theme which runs through the whole book: the idea that things have 'biographies'. This idea might initially strike you as somewhat strange – we are perhaps more used to the idea of biography as a genre of writing which helps us understand the lives of 'people', not 'things'. But in the same way that biography can help us to construct a narrative of a person's life and personal relationships, we shall suggest that it can also help us to tell the story of an object's history and, perhaps more important, its interrelationships with people and with other things. Biographies of particular individuals are usually structured around the familiar events of birth to death. These events form part of the life cycle of humans. Objects can also be seen to have life cycles, beginning with how they were first made and running through to their last or current state of existence. For example, the life cycle of an object such as a china plate on display in a museum has followed a sequence of life stages, starting with being made from raw clay and going on to being taken out of daily use and being conserved as a museum object. An individual plate may have a distinctive biography (it may have been created by a famous potter, then owned by a French monarch and finally donated to a museum by an American collector). The *life cycle* is a reminder of the many stages that objects go through in their historical existence; the detail of those stages makes up the *biography* of a particular object.

Before we explore these linked ideas, as we shall across the chapters in this book, this chapter will provide some background for them through a brief exploration of the origins of material culture and its study in late nineteenth- and early twentieth-century archaeology and anthropology museums. Many of the early techniques developed at that time by archaeologists and anthropologists in relation to Material Culture Studies remain important today. In other parts of this book, you will explore ways of describing, classifying and interpreting objects and their **context**s which have their origins in the work of scholars in museums over a century ago. While the module does not present a complete history of the development of Archaeology and Anthropology, this chapter will help you understand how and why these methods were developed during the nineteenth and early twentieth centuries, and their relationship to the concept of material culture more generally.

But before we begin to examine the history of studying material culture, and look at specific case studies which can help us understand the value, meaning and life cycles of objects, we should start by asking ourselves a simple yet fundamental question: what do we mean when we talk about material culture?

1.1 What is material culture?

We all live our lives as part of a network of material things. Some of these things might strike us as remarkable, but many of the things which we use to shape our world and which in turn shape us as humans as part of our everyday lives go unnoticed.

How did you start the day this morning? Like me, you might have started it to the sound of a digital clock-radio alarm, followed by a mug of tea in one hand and a bowl of cereal in the other. These objects – the clock-radio, the mug, the bowl – are unremarkable objects, in the sense that I use them every day and have given them very little thought since I first acquired them. Yet they are integral to defining who I am (both physically and socially) and act as a daily physical link between myself and the world. Here are some examples of how objects might connect me both to abstract structures like world trade and to intangible memories:

- Another human was involved in designing, making and selling these objects, so by owning them I am connected to the route these objects have already travelled and to the people behind those processes.

- I exercised some choice about how I acquired them (or kept them, if they were gifts), so I have made some design choices that reflect my interests and willingness to spend a little or a lot of money. These choices embrace new technology (the clock-radio), the beauty of a craft object (my handmade mug) and sentimental value (the bowl was a present).

- I use the objects in ways that go beyond the purely functional. So I might make someone else tea in the mug as a gesture of affection or friendship, show off my clock-radio to a visitor, and keep the bowl (even though it has a chip in it) because it cheers me up in the mornings.

These are examples of ways that we all, often unconsciously, use objects as things that 'speak', in the sense that they carry messages that can be decoded. They can be used to tell a story about me, but that story can be told only if we understand the objects themselves. Objects carry meanings that can be understood by people who habitually engage with these objects, or with similar types of objects. However, this book tackles the problem of how we can understand objects that are not necessarily familiar. They might be made in unfamiliar ways, for unknown uses, or have acquired new uses very different from their original purposes.

In recent decades, the academic disciplines that come together as the humanities have been increasingly interested in the cultural objects that help create social identities. Some of these disciplines have always been concerned with the study of objects such as works of art or classical buildings; others have developed methods that prioritise the study of texts, ranging from wills to diaries as well as literature. One important aim of this module is to give you insights into how the study of the humanities involves both texts and objects. In this book, the focus is on objects and on how the evidence from these objects' own qualities can be used to understand their place in human societies. After all, most objects are never written about – so future owners or finders are not likely to have a helpful text to explain why my old chipped bowl (probably dating from the 1980s) has evidence of continued use. This book gives you the tools to investigate objects, to relate them to human societies, and to think about how the objects provide evidence for their own meaning and significance. You may be more familiar with critical approaches to the written word and with looking for evidence within texts; for a character's motivation in a novel, for example. For both objects and texts, an academic approach needs the right methods (the tools) and appropriate theory (a framework for meaning) to create critical insights.

Objects are things that we and other societies interact with, attribute meaning to, and occasionally change the meanings of, as the objects evolve and the needs of their owners move on. When you understand how to work with objects, you will be able to start thinking of these things as source materials for your studies in the arts and humanities.

Activity

You should allow about 10 minutes for this activity.

Think about what you did in the last hour before beginning to read this chapter, and make a list of all of the objects which you used in that time. What does your list say to you about your relationship to things? How important are these relationships to the ways in which we live our lives and conduct our daily activities?

Discussion

In answering this question, I drew up a table, listing actions in the first column and the objects which were involved in them in the second. Because I wrote this in the morning, I thought back over the process of waking up and getting out of bed, taking a shower, drying myself with a towel, dressing, having breakfast, brushing my teeth and – because I was working from home this morning – walking into my home office and turning on my computer to start writing. So my table looked like this:

Action	Objects
Wake up	Bed (and indeed the bedroom and the flat that contains it, which might also be considered to be objects in their own right, as might the floor across which I walked to turn the doorknob to open the bedroom door)
Shower	Boiler, shower cubicle, showerhead, taps, shampoo, soap, towel
Dressing	Wardrobe and its contents
Breakfast	Pantry, refrigerator, kettle, mug, teabag, milk, cereal box, cereal bowl, spoon, chair, table
Brush teeth	Sink, tap, tube of toothpaste, toothbrush
Start working	Chair, table, telephone line, computer, monitor, keyboard, mouse, books, pen, notebook

My first reaction when looking back at this list was surprise at the sheer number of objects involved in the simple operation of starting my day. But my list of objects also very much defines me as an Anglophone living in the early twenty-first century in the city of London. My use of many of these objects – such as soap – would be shared by many people living across the contemporary world. However, parts of my list would be very different for people living in different times and places. If I was waking up in a village in Myanmar (Burma), for example, I might be using different utensils to prepare and eat my breakfast, and I might have chosen to eat rice instead of breakfast cereal. And if I was waking up in London in the thirteenth century, my list of objects would be even more different and definitely much shorter.

I have also kept my list fairly neutral, in that I have not described the objects beyond naming them. If I added the brand (and date of manufacture) of each object – if, for instance, I said my computer was the latest Apple Mac, and if you either really loved this brand or hated it – your own reading of my list might create additional responses. The more description we add to objects, the more we are defining them in selected ways. This is the next important point for this book: that description (attaching words to objects) is rarely neutral, because it involves the selection of characteristics and the interpretation of their significance. Attaching words to objects, then, needs to be approached with the same level of critical scrutiny that you would use when trying to describe the significance of a poem.

The objects you will encounter in this chapter go far beyond a mug and breakfast bowl in England in 2014. The study of objects in terms of their cultural significance began in western academic terms several centuries ago. This chapter discusses two academic disciplines that emerged during the nineteenth century in western universities: Archaeology and Anthropology. Archaeology was developed in order to try to understand the distant past, particularly in relation to societies that have left objects but not texts. Archaeologists devised methods and theories to understand a range of different types of evidence, but it is the study of objects made or modified by people that is the focus of the chapters in this book. Objects could be collected and displayed in museums, as a means of illustrating the human past. Also during the nineteenth century, interest in living cultures encountered through western colonisation increased as it seemed likely that such societies might become extinct. The objects used by living cultures were also collected to be displayed in museums, illustrating the diversity of human societies up to the present. Anthropology developed as the study of cultures across the world with a strong interest in making comparisons between cultures. This emphasis on evidence from the objects produced by societies explains why the humanities call the study of objects in society 'material culture'. While the physics behind a physical object, and the technology that makes an object possible, are interesting and relevant, they are not the prime focus of study. It is the human creation and uses of objects that define material culture.

1.2 The 'origin' of material culture

The study of material culture uses methods and theories that have been developed to answer questions about the relationships of humans to objects. The origins of the term 'material culture' lie in the emergence of academic ways of studying material objects, initially those from past societies and then those from living societies, that were developed during the nineteenth century. The motivation for such studies came from the realisation that historical documents could not answer fundamental questions about the origins and development of modern humans. The academic disciplines discussed in this section have changed considerably in their methods and approaches since the nineteenth century, but the fascination of observing ourselves remains and speaks to very basic questions about what it is to be human.

Anthropology: the study of living societies

In the nineteenth century, western nations consolidated their territorial expansion through colonisation across the world. Older trade routes were turned into permanent colonial pathways that extended into larger areas than had previously been explored by westerners. Encounters with new societies with radically different ways of organising social relations, belief-systems and technologies provoked systematic research into documenting the varieties of human culture. The chronology for the human past was being dramatically extended back tens if not hundreds of thousands of years by archaeological discoveries. The first anthropologists began to compare living societies in order to develop a sense of the global variation in human cultures.

Public museums, which had originated in the eighteenth century, increasingly opened up galleries to display objects sent back from new colonies (Buchli, 2002). Much of the evidence drawn on by Anthropology came from understanding the role of objects in societies. The first anthropologists observed societies whose technology was unrelated to the western experience of industrialisation and who had very limited contact with western economic systems of value. The objects that these societies produced defied existing western ideas about beauty, had functions not easily compared with western uses of objects, and seemed to be employed in social rituals that had no parallels in European practices. How could they be understood?

The answers gradually emerged from existing scientific habits of classifying data. Methods of breaking down complex phenomena like plants into component parts, and comparing their features, had proved essential in finding ways of ordering masses of potential data into easily compared categories. Carl Linnaeus (1707–1778) was the Swedish botanist who developed the modern scheme which is used to name and distinguish between different plant and animal species (see Figure 1.1). This system of classification is called taxonomy, and it underpins our ability to name and describe new species and to place them in an orderly relationship with already known species. The taxonomic schemes which were developed in the biological sciences during the eighteenth century formed models for the development, during the nineteenth century, of similar schemes for ordering human societies based on the relative complexity of their technology (or material culture). You may already realise that a western sense of relative complexity would inevitably prioritise western understandings of what was complex. Despite this, the nineteenth-century collectors of material culture really needed to look closely at objects in order to begin to find ways of describing and comparing unfamiliar creations.

What is Anthropology?

Anthropology, in its broadest sense, refers to the study of humans. It is concerned with understanding what it means to be human in both a biological and a social sense. Nowadays, the discipline is divided into separate fields, so Physical Anthropology explores the biological, and often genetic, aspects of cultural groups, while Social Anthropology studies social structures and material culture.

Anthropologists collect their data through the method of **ethnography**, the observation of a society's use of objects, rituals and other activities and how the participants explain the meaning and significance of their culture. Objects collected from ethnographic studies that are put on display in museums are often called ethnographic displays or collections.

You should allow about 15 minutes for this activity.

Activity

Linnaeus' taxonomic scheme in Figure 1.1 is written in Latin, which was still the shared language of science in the eighteenth century. The table

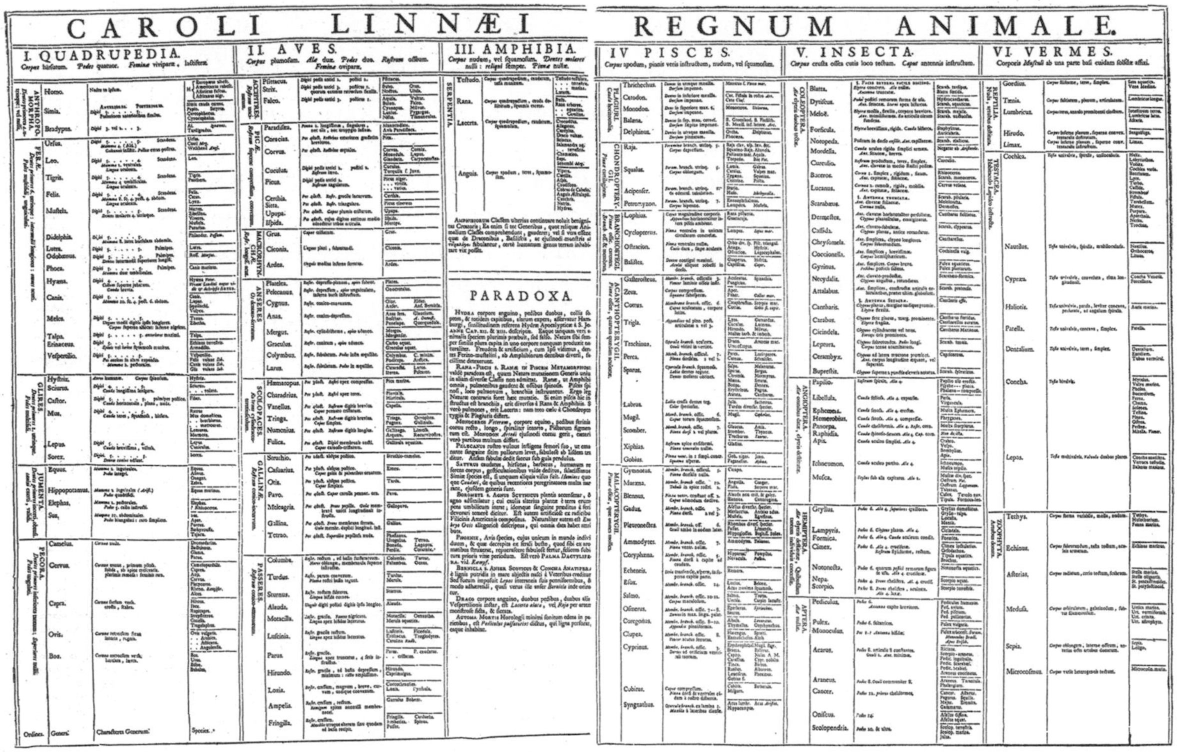
CAROLI LINNÆI REGNUM ANIMALE.

I. QUADRUPEDIA. II. AVES. III. AMPHIBIA. IV. PISCES. V. INSECTA. VI. VERMES.

PARADOXA

Figure 1.1 Table of the animal kingdom (*regnum animale*), from the first edition of Carl Linnaeus(1735) *Systema Naturæ*. The headings in this table read: 'four-legged', 'birds', 'amphibians', 'fish', 'insects' and 'worms'

is set out as six columns, which divide the 'animal kingdom' (*regnum animale*) into distinct groups: 'four-legged' (*quadrupedia*), 'birds' (*aves*), 'amphibians' (*amphibian*), 'fish' (*pisces*), 'insects' (*insecta*) and 'worms' (*vermes*). Under each group heading, you can see that there are four columns, and reading from left to right, more and more information appears within the columns. The columns represent a progressive breaking down of the main groups into sub-groups: by order, then genus (with another column to describe these genera), then species. You may be familiar with how family trees are laid out, as a series of branches into subdivisions to show how your ancestors ultimately connect with you. Linnaeus created similar subdivisions to demonstrate connections within groups, but also to show differences between them.

Using this model of breaking down groups into characteristics, think of a class of objects that you are familiar with that you could apply this method to. For example, you might try this with cooking equipment or with a wardrobe of clothes.

Discussion

I thought about this in relation to my cooking equipment and it works reasonably well. My top-level classification would be divided into two 'orders', or groups, of electrical and non-electrical, then each of those groups could be divided according to their main material, as 'genera': metal, glass, pottery, wood and plastic. A 'species' would be an item within one of these genera; for example, a wooden spoon. A wooden fruit bowl would be a different species within the same genus as the wooden spoon. If I owned both a bread-maker and a deep-fat fryer, they could be categorised as the same species, as the subdivisions would be: electrical (order), metal (genus), metal box with a heating element (species). Anyone who wasn't a keen cook could probably follow this scheme for sorting my kitchen contents without having to know exactly what each item was used for. This descriptive classification is the attraction of the biological taxonomic scheme both for Anthropology and, as you will read next, for Archaeology.

Archaeology: the study of ancient things

The term 'archaeology' comes from the Greek for ancient history; as a discipline, Archaeology developed as a means of recovering the physical remains of societies that had often existed before the advent of written records. Archaeology is largely defined by its attention to the material culture of societies, in contrast to the discipline of History, which prioritises the written record as evidence. In broad terms, the early archaeologists developed methods for relating objects found in the ground to the relative sequence in time of their existence: objects found in layers nearest the ground surface were younger than objects found below them, because they were made and used and then abandoned more recently. Put like that, this may sound obvious, but it was an essential realisation for understanding how a site with many layers of use evolved over time. Early archaeologists working in the early nineteenth century had not only to solve the problem of how to date objects, but also to find methods to help them understand the objects from one site in relation to other sites (Trigger, 1996).

In the 1820s, the Danish scholar Christian Jürgensen Thomsen (1788–1865) developed the 'three-age system' in order to classify archaeological artefacts into a chronological and technological sequence of Stone Age, Bronze Age and Iron Age. Thomsen observed that stone tools tended to appear in the lowest levels of prehistoric sites, with bronze items lying above them and finally iron objects apparent in the upper layers. He used his three-age system as a way of dating archaeological sites relative to one another based on the materials contained within them, and as a new way of arranging artefacts in a museum's collection. Thomsen's three-age system allowed archaeologists confidently to compare stone tools, on the basis of a shared technology, and to begin to analyse the characteristics of groups of stones shaped for cutting, or hammering, or piercing holes. Although archaeologists could not see these tools in use, as an anthropologist might be able to observe with a living society, they could begin to move towards deductions about the functions and changing manufacture of the tools, and thus about how the stone-tool-using humans might have been living.

This attention to technology in the past provided a means to put archaeological sites and their finds into an order. Figure 1.2 shows how Thomsen's classification of tools by their material was used by another archaeologist, John Lubbock (1834–1913), to put archaeological sites

	STONE.					BRONZE.								IRON.							COINS.
	Axes.	Arrows.	Flakes.	Other Objects	Total.	Axes.	Knives.	Lances.	Sickles.	Fish Hooks.	Ornaments.	Sundries.	Total.	Swords.	Axes.	Knives.	Lances.	Ornaments.	Sundries.	Total.	
SWITZERLAND. Wangen	1500	...	2500	450	4450	...	...	...	...	...	...	...	...	...	...	...	...	...	...	...	0
Moosseedorf	100	25	2300	277	2702	...	...	...	...	...	...	...	...	...	...	...	...	...	...	...	0
Nussdorf	1000	100	100	30	1230	...	...	...	...	...	...	...	...	...	...	...	...	...	...	...	0
Wauwyl	43	36	200	147	426	...	...	...	...	...	...	...	...	...	...	...	...	...	...	...	0
Nidau	33	?	?	335 Corn-crushers ?	368	23	102	27	18	109	1420	305	2004	...	..	...	...	...	...	...	0
Cortaillod	?	?	?	?		13	22	4	2	71	515	208	835	...	...	...	...	...	...	...	0
Estavayer	?	?	?	?		6	14	...	1	43	403	150	617	...	...	...	...	...	...	...	0
Corcelettes	?	?	?	?		1	19	2	7	...	465	16	510	...	...	...	...	...	...	...	0
Morges	0	?	?	Many Corn-crushers		50	20	11	11	10	108	?	210	...	...	...	...	... More than 100	1	1	0
Marin	...	...	Some.	12 Balls		1 Pierced	...	...	...	...	1	13	15	50	5	4	23	more than 100	61	250	9
DENMARK. Nydam	...	...	...	A few Whet-stones		...	...	...	...	...	...	Ornaments very numerous	...	100	30	86	500 at least	?	300 at least	1000 at least	34

Figure 1.2 Table from John Lubbock (1865) *Pre-historic Times*, London, William and Norgate. The table shows the division of a series of European archaeological sites into 'Stone', 'Bronze' and 'Iron' Ages, based on the presence or absence of particular types of artefacts made using different raw materials

into groups, according to the objects they contained. At the same time, the comparison of past technology with the achievements of the nineteenth-century Industrial Revolution tended to encourage scholars to think in terms of a primitive past leading in a smooth and inevitable path to their own time (Bennett, 2004). In reality, progress is now understood to follow a more complex and less inevitable trajectory. But the nineteenth-century archaeological contribution to the study of **cultural evolution** did help to make the ordering of objects central to the study of human culture.

Typological approaches: Pitt Rivers and the rise of museum anthropology

The early archaeologists and anthropologists were researching human evolution by looking outwards at other cultures that were outside of western industrialisation, but not looking back at themselves to see if ethnography could help to investigate their own society. The study of industrial societies by their own inhabitants became the discipline of Sociology, while modern Archaeology and Anthropology do now also investigate western material culture. However, the early approaches to material culture were compelling achievements on their own terms, and a spectacular example of how objects could be collected and grouped scientifically still survives at the Pitt Rivers Museum, owned by the University of Oxford.

Augustus Henry Lane Fox Pitt Rivers (1827–1890) was a wealthy man who was able to follow his fascination with objects through Archaeology and through collecting weaponry from diverse human cultures, as well as other items such as stone tools, pottery, clothing, personal ornaments and religious figures. After inheriting the Rivers estate and title in 1882, Pitt Rivers devoted his life to archaeological excavation. He developed a new method for cataloguing excavated artefacts, which would become extremely influential in the development of modern Archaeology (Gosden and Larson, 2007).

Pitt Rivers kept his extensive collection in his own home, but later donated it to the University of Oxford's Natural History Museum. The curators agreed to organise the exhibits according to Pitt Rivers' own arrangement, based on theories of cultural evolution. This differs from the taxonomies that organised objects by material (stone, bronze, iron) because it used different categories based on the function of objects. Pitt Rivers brought together groups of objects from different cultures which he perceived to represent different stages of cultural evolution.

These groups dealt with a particular artefact 'type' or theme – for example 'spears', or 'the treatment of the dead'. The priority he gave to types of object (knives, arrows, beakers) is called the typological method (the classification of things according to their characteristics). These groups are called type series. Bringing types of object together across cultures was intended to demonstrate how humans had moved through various stages of cultural evolution, using Linnaean taxonomy (Figure 1.1) as a model, as Pitt Rivers himself explained:

> Human ideas, as represented by the various products of human industry, are capable of classification into genera, species, and varieties, in the same manner as the products of the vegetable and animal kingdoms, and in their development from the homogeneous to the heterogeneous they obey the same laws.

> (Pitt Rivers, 1875, p. 307)

The important point in this theory of cultural evolution is that it suggests a model of progress that all human societies should pass through over time, in order to achieve the most complex level of evolution (that of western industrial society). The theory does not allow for societies to pursue a variety of ways of expressing cultural complexity, and so it is described as a unilinear model: it follows only one pathway. Objects were arranged according to sequences which showed their 'evolution' from simple, 'primitive' forms to more complex, 'advanced' ones. Figure 1.3 is a published drawing of items laid out in a very similar way to how Pitt Rivers' objects were displayed in the museum. It shows two views of each object, a stone tool drawn face-down and from the side. The drawing can be understood from left to right, showing that each tool changes in size and level of finish. Pitt Rivers ignored place and date of manufacture and assumed the same function (a cutting tool like an axe) for each object. He created his own series based on visual comparison, and interpreted the results as evidence of 'transition' or progress in technology.

Activity

You should now complete the online activity 'Pitt Rivers and the type series', which you can find on the Study Planner of the module website. This activity, based on Pitt Rivers' work, gives you the opportunity to sort a series of objects into a type series.

You should allow about 30 minutes for this activity.

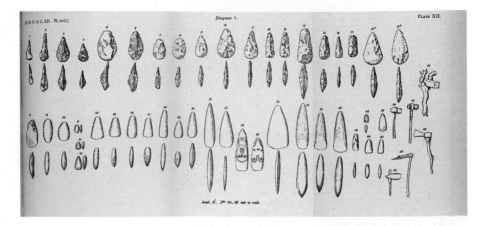

Figure 1.3   A series of stone tools 'of the same type from nearly every part of the globe', showing a sequence of the transition from flaked-stone hand axes to polished-stone 'celts', *c.*1867. From A.H.L.F. Pitt Rivers (1906) *The Evolution of Culture and Other Essays*, Oxford, Clarendon Press. © The British Library Board, London

If you tried the online activity, you might have concluded that getting the objects into the sequence set up by Pitt Rivers did not prove that the sequence was 'right'; it simply showed that your visual comparisons were, intuitively, similar to those made by Pitt Rivers. Photographs of the Pitt Rivers Museum at the time show the arrangement of each type series in different cabinets, or according to sequence along the walls of the museum (see Figure 1.4). This method of arrangement was influential in suggesting that objects could be successfully analysed in terms of their own qualities (material, form, manufacture, function) and ordered according to western science.

Unfortunately, today this method is as discredited as the theory of unilinear cultural evolution. The method and the theory are mutually reinforcing: western science creates an order based on western scientific principles and finds evidence to support western cultural complexity ahead of all the other objects in each type series. The method of interrogating the objects in terms of their technological qualities ignores all the other possible data. For living societies, this would include assessing the objects in use, in their social settings, with their full range of meanings. Material culture research cannot take place solely in a museum glass case.

The theory is now discredited partly because it has no explanatory power to account for the nature of cultural change. You might reflect that the idea of inevitable progress is still a widespread belief within

Figure 1.4 South side of the Pitt Rivers Museum, Oxford, c.1895–1901. Photographer unknown. Pitt Rivers Museum, Oxford, 1999.19.1. Photo: © Pitt Rivers Museum, Oxford. Note the series of spears, lances, knives and other weapons displayed in sequence along the wall on the top level of the museum, and the way in which 'types' of objects are displayed together regardless of geographical origin or time period

western economies, but you are now aware that modern scholarship does not use linear evolution as a model to explain differences between societies.

Early Anthropology and the Benin bronzes

The West African kingdom of Benin (now in modern Nigeria) was colonised by the British in a process that resulted in 1897 in the destruction of Benin City and the looting of artworks known as the Benin bronzes. If you have studied AA100 *The arts past and present*, you will be familiar with this. The bronze plaques were sought after by museums and private collectors, including the Pitt Rivers Museum and the British Museum, which put 300 plaques on display in 1897.

Since the 1880s the British Museum had been organising its collections according to the latest anthropological theories of the development of cultures. The Benin bronzes added to the evidence for how societies progressed along the pathway from 'savagery to civilisation' (Loftus and Wood, 2008, p. 51). However, the excellence of the bronzes (said to be as good as Italian Renaissance bronze casting) was problematic in the context of the living society they were taken from, which British reports treated as violent and degraded in practising human sacrifice. How could beautiful and complex objects come from such a society? Anthropologists debated whether they were the result of early European contact (Pitt Rivers argued that such contact had been made by Portuguese traders in the sixteenth century), or made in Africa without European influence. The theory of unilinear cultural evolution could not easily account for the Benin bronzes. Although the British Museum curators concluded from a range of evidence that the Benin bronzes were made without European contact, the dominant account became that the Benin makers had learned from the Portuguese and that their techniques had subsequently degenerated (Loftus and Wood, 2008, pp. 52–3).

The value of the Benin bronzes in European museums extended beyond academic research into the past. National museums were also seen as resources for understanding colonised societies. Societies that were represented as weak and undeveloped could be presented as being helped by the arrival of western systems of government and of Christianity. In turn, anthropologists' explanations of colonised societies could help colonial administrators understand their new subjects.

Contextual approaches: Boas, Malinowski and the demise of museum anthropology

The early part of the twentieth century saw a move away from the *museum* (and material culture) to the *field* (and observations of human social behaviour) as the focus of anthropological interest in the study of human societies, while the mission of Anthropology shifted from collecting objects to collecting observations of other cultures.

The demise of museum anthropology is often attributed to the work of anthropologist Franz Boas (1858–1942), who rejected the evolutionary models of culture and developed the contextual or relativistic approach. Boas was a German-American anthropologist who undertook ethnographic fieldwork with Inuit people in Canada and among indigenous north Pacific coast groups during the 1880s and 1890s. His direct involvement with different indigenous groups during these periods of intensive fieldwork caused him to question the dominant model of cultural evolution. Instead, he emphasised the ways in which items of material culture which appeared similar in form might be developed in different contexts to address different problems within different human societies (Boas, 1940, 1887; Conn, 1998, p. 108).

In contrast to Pitt Rivers' museum displays of type series, Boas created displays that prioritised the people behind the objects. As a curator at the American Museum of Natural History in New York City, he oversaw the development of the Hall of Northwest Coast Indian culture, using the opportunity to demonstrate how such an exhibit could be organised along contextual, rather than **evolutionary** principles. Boas had the artefacts in the gallery, named the North Pacific Hall, organised according to **provenance** (the place where they had originated) in the first instance, ensuring that materials from particular groups were displayed together so that the ways in which they functioned together in a specific context could be understood by the viewer (Jacknis, 1985). A number of 'life groups' were installed, consisting of mannequins posed to demonstrate the ways in which objects were worn or used together. These were often staged to demonstrate both the manufacture and the use of artefacts, and to represent both male and female subsistence activities. These new principles for the ordering and display of museum exhibits reflected Boas' beliefs that objects could only be understood within their individual cultural context (see Figures 1.5 and 1.6), and not abstracted from it. Today we use the term **cultural relativism** to describe this way of thinking. A quick comparison with the images showing Pitt Rivers' type series of objects (for example,

Figure 1.5 The North Pacific Hall from the south, *c.*1902. Photographed by E.G. Keller. American Museum of Natural History, New York, 351. Photo: © American Museum of Natural History Library, New York. This photograph shows the utilisation of mannequins to demonstrate artefacts in use, according to Boas' scheme

Figure 1.4) should show you how different Boas' contextual displays were.

In 1905 Boas became the head of the first Department of Anthropology at Columbia University in New York. He continued to criticise museum anthropology, suggesting that the appropriate centre for the discipline was the university, rather than the museum. At the same time, anthropological research practices placed increasing emphasis on **participant observation** (the researcher takes part in the lives of a society or social group rather than remaining in the background) and on the observation and description of *human behaviour* in preference to *objects*. Another way of thinking of this is to see it as a shift in emphasis

Figure 1.6 The North Pacific Hall from the south, *c.*1910. Photographer unknown. American Museum of Natural History, New York, 33003. Photo: © American Museum of Natural History Library, New York. This photograph belongs to the period after Boas' involvement in the museum, but clearly shows his influence on the arrangement of its exhibits, with objects from particular tribal groups assembled and displayed together, and a large life exhibit occupying the central part of the hall

from the indirect study of humans by way of their material culture in museums, towards the more direct study of human cultures in the field itself.

One of the most influential figures in the development of the participant observation method of anthropological fieldwork was the Polish anthropologist Bronisław Malinowski (1884–1942), who most famously undertook fieldwork in the Trobriand Islands early in the twentieth century. In his monograph based on this work, *Argonauts of the Western Pacific* (1922), Malinowski wrote that the task of the ethnographer is to 'grasp the native's point of view, his relation to life, to realize his vision of his world' (1922, p. 25). Malinowski learned the language of the Trobriand Islanders and spent long periods living with them, so that he could immerse himself in their culture and understand not only objects, but also people's cultural traditions and behaviour,

Figure 1.7 Bronisław Malinowski seated with a group of men in the Trobriand Islands, *c.*1915. Photographer unknown. The London School of Economics and Political Science, London, MALINOWSKI/3/18/5. Photo: © The Library of the London School of Economics and Political Science

within their own context (see Figure 1.7). In many ways this was the realisation of Boas' cultural relativism and the way it could be applied to Anthropology. This method of research – participant observation – came to be the dominant method of anthropological research over the coming decades. We shall return to Malinowski's work in the Trobriand Islands in the next section of this chapter.

1.3 The Kula cycle

Malinowski's work in the Trobriand Islands includes a case study on a particular ritual called the Kula cycle. This case study has helped generate some valuable ways of understanding how objects carry meaning and acquire histories through how they are used, showing how western assumptions about what objects mean do not provide all the possible answers. The case study demonstrates how the contextual approach allows the owners of the objects to explain their understanding of their own actions. The ritual that uses the objects has a crucial role in maintaining social relations between the island communities, but it operates outside western categories of economic value and away from the unspoken rules that westerners are familiar

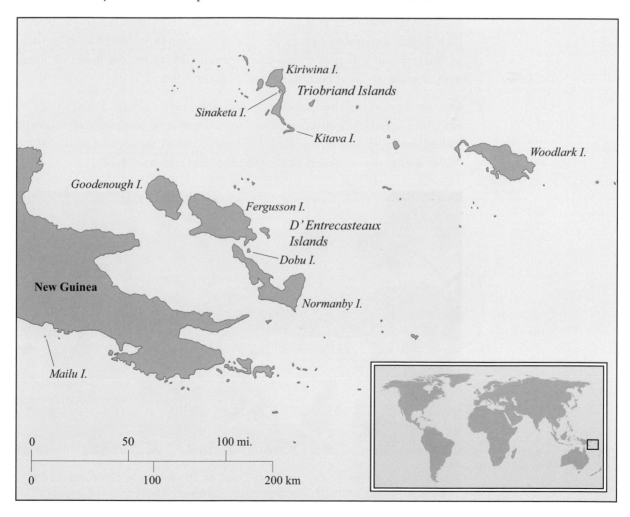

Figure 1.8 Map of Trobriand Islands

with about making a gift to someone. The people who perform the ritual also own its meaning. In addition, this case study shows us objects in action, as things that move and gain additional meanings as a result.

Malinowski began his work of participation in the Trobriand Islands (Figure 1.8) during the First World War. He observed a series of rituals associated with the **exchange** of two objects, which fascinated him. This exchange system was called Kula. The Kula cycle, which continues today, encompasses more than a dozen different island groups of the Massim archipelago of Papua New Guinea, involving thousands of individuals who traditionally travelled great distances for up to months at a time to take part in the ritualised exchanges (Leach and Leach, 1983).

Malinowski observed that every few months Trobriand Islanders used their highly decorated canoes to visit other islands in order to take part in feasting and gift giving and to exchange and barter for items of local manufacture or local resources (see Figures 1.9 and 1.10).

During these visits the islanders would attempt to obtain Kula valuables – red shell-disc necklaces (called *veigun* or *soulava*, and made of *Spondylus* shells) and white shell armbands (called *mwali*, and made of *Conus* shells) – from each other (see Figures 1.11 and 1.12).

Figure 1.9 A gathering of men from Dobu on the beach at Sinaketa, in the Trobriand Islands, *c*.1915. Photographer unknown. The London School of Economics and Political Science, London, MALINOWSKI/3/19/10. Photo: © The Library of the London School of Economic and Political Science

Figure 1.10 Intricately carved prow designs on Dobuan canoes at Sinaketa, in the Trobriand Islands, *c.*1915. Photographer unknown. The London School of Economics and Political Science, London, MALINOWSKI/3/19/9. Photo: © The Library of the London School of Economics and Political Science

Figure 1.11 A group of *Mwali* armbands brought from Kitava to Omaraka in the Trobriand Islands, *c.*1915. Photographer unknown. The London School of Economics and Political Science, London, MALINOWSKI/3/ARG/60. Photo: © The Library of the London School of Economic and Political Science

He observed that these valuables were traded in a cycle (hence 'Kula cycle'), with red shell-disc necklaces being traded from trading partners on one set of islands to another, circling the islands in a clockwise direction, and white shell armbands (or armlets) being traded and circling in a counterclockwise direction (see Figure 1.13). The terms of

Figure 1.12 An example of *Mwali*, a *Conus* shell armband believed to have been used in the Kula exchanges of the Trobriand Islands. Pitt Rivers Museum, Oxford, 1933.40.18. Photo: © Pitt Rivers Museum, Oxford

the exchange were strictly controlled according to specific rules and customs.

Kula valuables have no function other than as prestige items. They have no monetary value and cannot be used to purchase other goods. They are not bartered but are given as 'gifts', with the status of the giver being increased by the generosity displayed in the act of giving. Generally speaking, the gift of one or more Kula valuable(s) immediately results in a counter-gift of the other form of valuable, and may also result in future exchanges of Kula valuables and other items. When Kula valuables are exchanged, the receiver is also given the detailed histories of each object's previous owners, and Kula valuables become more important depending on the status of their previous owners and the length of time they have been involved in the cycle. The importance of the Kula cycle is not only to gain individual prestige for the givers and receivers, but also because the cycle provides opportunities for the movement and exchange of other objects, ideas, customs and accompanying social interactions.

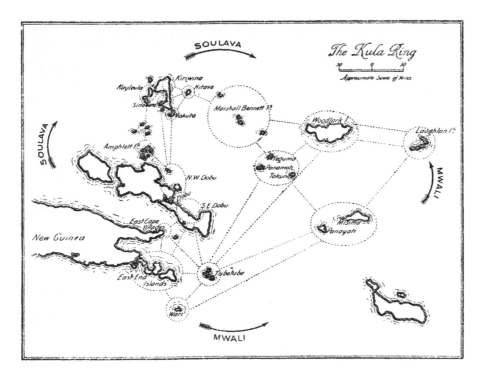

Figure 1.13 The Kula ring and the direction of trade of the two forms of Kula valuables. From Bronisław Malinowski (1922) *Argonauts of the Western Pacific*, London, Routledge and Kegan Paul. The scale shows 30-mile (48-km) intervals. Subsequent research has demonstrated that the Kula ring spans 18 island communities of the Massim archipelago, an area of some 780 square kilometres (300 square miles)

Activity

Now watch the film 'Malinowski and the Kula cycle', which you can find on the module website. This is an extract from the BBC documentary *Tales from the Jungle: Malinowski* (first broadcast in 2007), which focuses on the work of Malinowski in the context of the history of Anthropology.

The film lasts about 7 minutes, but you should allow about 30 minutes for this activity.

Kula valuables are described in the film as having no 'function' or utilitarian purpose. While they might not have any immediate practical purpose for the individuals who use them, can you think what their function may be at a broader, social level? Can you think of any objects that we use in our own society which have no practical function or purpose?

Discussion

The discussion of Kula valuables reminded me of various family heirlooms which have been handed down to me and which have no specific use-value but are nonetheless very important in defining who I am, and in my sense of my own place within my family's history. Clearly the 'function' of an object is not limited to its utility or use-value: objects also have symbolic values and function as ambassadors in social networks of exchange. Another example of this type of object is the gifts which are given to heads of state when they visit other countries – the objects themselves are unlikely to get much use, but they have symbolic values and are bound up in social networks of exchange and **reciprocity** (informal systems of exchange).

You will have come up with your own examples, but I hope you can see from this discussion that objects are caught up in complex social webs and that their function lies not only in their use-value or utility – it is also social and symbolic.

1.4 Object biographies

We have seen that Malinowski's work on the Kula cycle suggested ways in which individual objects might have distinct biographies as a result of their movement from one context to the next – in this case, the movement of a gift from one person to another. The *Oxford English Dictionary online* (which you can access through the OU Library website) gives three definitions of the word 'biography':

1   The process of recording the events and circumstances of another person's life, esp. for publication (latterly in any of various written, recorded, or visual media); the documenting of individual life histories (and, later, other forms of thematic historical narrative), considered as a genre of writing or social history.

2   A written account of the life of an individual, esp. a historical or public figure; (also) a brief profile of a person's life or work. Later more generally: a themed narrative history of a specific subject in any of various written, recorded, or visual media.

3   Personal history; the events or circumstances of a person's life, viewed collectively. Also: the course of an individual human life, or the life cycle of an animal or plant.

(*Oxford English Dictionary*, 2010)

These three definitions have two important features in common. First, biographies relate to a *specific* person. Second, biographies are produced in the form of a narrative history which tracks a person's life trajectory *historically, through time.*

But what if we were to take this model of a biography and apply it to a 'thing'? The model might be applied more broadly to help us understand the social function of things. In a volume called *The Social Life of Things*, the socio-cultural anthropologist Arjun Appadurai (1986) has written about the ways in which objects move about in society and change meaning depending on their context within local and global systems. To track these transformations, he suggests we should study the 'paths' and 'life histories' of things. In the same book, the anthropologist Igor Kopytoff argues that a biographical approach to objects should ask the same questions of objects which a biographer would ask of a person. In addition to thinking about its status and the ways that an object gives rank and standing to its owner, we should ask:

> Where does the thing come from and who made it? What has been its career so far, and what do people consider to be an ideal career for such things? What are the recognized 'ages' or periods in the thing's 'life', and what are the cultural markers for them? How does the thing's use change with its age, and what happens to it when it reaches the end of its usefulness?

(Kopytoff, 1986, pp. 66–7)

The emphasis in Kopytoff's work on when and where we encounter an object is important. It draws our attention to the fact that the ways in which humans relate to any individual object shift, depending on the contexts within which they are encountered or found together.

Anthropologist Janet Hoskins, author of *Biographical Objects: How Things Tell the Stories of People's Lives* (1998), has distinguished two different kinds of approach to object biography (Hoskins, 2006). The first is called an **object-driven approach**, which is most dominant within Anthropology. It starts with ethnographic research and builds a story around the ways in which particular objects are perceived by the people they are linked to – the makers, users, consumers or viewers of those objects. Malinowski's way of writing his study of the Kula cycle was an object-driven approach (although he did not intend to create object biographies). Object-driven approaches tend to use groups of objects, rather than single objects.

The second approach, which is more often that of the archaeologist, historian or art historian, is to start with the object itself and try to build a context for it by using written sources such as diaries, inventories or other documentary records (where they survive), or by examining the associations of objects with one another and with the context in which they are found in the ground or on the surface (as is most often the case in Archaeology). This is the **object-centred approach**, which might focus on one object and use methods of close visual analysis to tease out its form and characteristics, before following up the visual clues with evidence from other contexts. Using this approach, art experts might suggest, for example, that a painting of an unknown man is actually a rare image of William Shakespeare (see Chapter 4). Object-centred approaches usually work with one or a small group of similar objects, often without the benefit of seeing the object in its original social setting. The next two case studies work with object biographies in contrasting types of object: a nineteenth-century Australian Aboriginal tool and violins made by Stradivarius.

The biography of a flaked-glass Kimberley Point

This case study is of a Kimberley Point, a 'stone' tool made using bottle glass, which found its way into the Pitt Rivers Museum over a hundred years ago (see Figure 1.14). It features within an object biography which draws on the combination of both object-driven and object-centred approaches, through an exploration of particular documentary records as well as more generalised ethnographic information about how an object was used.

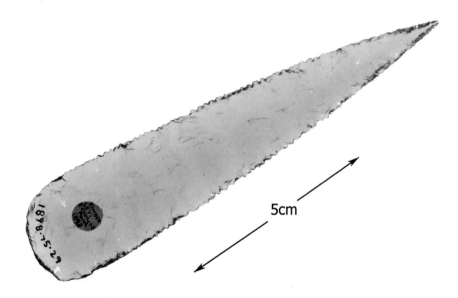

5cm

Figure 1.14 A flaked-glass Kimberley Point, *c.*1898. Pitt Rivers Museum, Oxford, 1898.75.29. Photo: © Pitt Rivers Museum, Oxford

The object is made of olive-green bottle glass, chipped into the shape of a spearhead of the kind produced by Aboriginal people from the Kimberley region of northwestern Australia. It has a museum label recording its unique catalogue number (an accession number), which is 1898.75.29, and a round sticker which reads 'Kimberley, E. Clement, Perth 1898'. Using the accession number, I was able to check the object entry in the museum accession book, which identifies it as one of four glass Kimberley Points sold to the museum by the collector Emile

Clement (1844–1928) along with another 109 ethnographic specimens from northwestern Australia, for which the museum paid £11 in the year 1898. It is one of at least 24 Kimberley spearheads, most of them made using glass, which were obtained by the Pitt Rivers Museum over the period 1898–1953 (Harrison, 2010).

Clement (see Figure 1.15) was a naturalist, mining engineer and collector who made at least three trips to Western Australia over the period 1895–1900, during which time he amassed a large collection of

Figure 1.15 Emile Clement and his wife, Emily Elizabeth Clement (née Morgan), Hove, *c.*1922. Photographer unknown. Photo: © Mr John Clement

ethnographic and botanical specimens which he sold to museums and collectors throughout the UK and continental Europe. By the time of his death in 1928, he had sold over 1600 Aboriginal artefacts to museums in the UK and continental Europe. We know something of his collecting activities, as in 1904 he published a series of notes and ethnographic observations, along with a catalogue of the objects he collected, in a short treatise (Clement, 1904).

It seems likely that this particular object was collected during the first or second of Clement's trips to Western Australia. But who made the object, and how? And why was this object, shaped like a stone spearhead, made using bottle glass? In the absence of any further specific documentary or physical evidence, it is not possible to say precisely who made the point. The object biography can be enhanced if we use the evidence available for other Kimberley Points to consider this particular object's life before it came into the hands of Clement. We know from archaeological evidence and other historical and ethnographic accounts that a Kimberley Point was a specialised stone tool form, requiring the use of a bone, wooden or (later) iron indenter to remove the very fine flakes across the surface of the artefact: a highly

Figure 1.16 Aboriginal man pressure-flaking glass using a metal indenter, *c.*1979. Photographed by Richard Woldendorp. State Library of Western Australia, Perth, 215845PD. Photo: State Library of Western Australia, reproduced with the permission of the Library Board of Western Australia

Figure 1.17 Aboriginal men at Moola Bulla Aboriginal Station, southeast Kimberley, Western Australia, *c.*1919. Photographer unknown. State Library of Western Australia, Perth, BL70656P. Photo: State Library of Western Australia, reproduced with the permission of the Library Board of Western Australia. The men are holding spears tipped with Kimberley Points

skilled operation which gives the spearhead its finely worked appearance (see Figure 1.16). Such points began to be manufactured, in an isolated area of Australia's northwest, only about one millennium before Europeans first settled in Australia. In the past they appear to have functioned as spearheads, hafted on to wooden spears (see Figure 1.17), but in the nineteenth and early twentieth centuries they more often appeared in symbolic gift exchanges between Aboriginal groups and in trade with colonial collectors.

After Aboriginal people from northwestern Australia came into contact with Europeans, these points became progressively more formalised in their shape, grew in length and were more and more finely worked at the precise time that their function as spearheads became far less relevant due to the availability of steel and guns. They were increasingly manufactured using European bottle glass as a raw material, which allowed for the manufacture of larger points but which made them functionally less useful as spearheads, as they were fragile and broke easily. They also appear, rather contradictorily, to have been made in the greatest numbers on settlements and reserves associated with Europeans, where food rations were being provided to Aboriginal people and there would have been less need for them as spearheads for hunting land game. Within the Aboriginal groups that manufactured them, points acquired new meanings as symbols of masculine status at the same time that their role as functional spearheads was being diminished. The introduction of bottle glass as a new raw material for making points meant that young men (they were only ever made by initiated men) could bypass traditional power structures (sources of stone were controlled by older, more powerful men). Men made these points as a symbol of their hunting prowess, but also to trade with Europeans. These glass spearheads were collected widely in colonial Australia as curios and souvenirs, and circulated in large numbers among museums and collectors across the globe in the early twentieth century (Harrison, 2006).

We now have some background information with which to construct an object biography describing the manufacture of this particular point and how it made its way into the museum. This glass point was probably made by an Aboriginal man living on or in close contact with a cattle-ranching station or mission in northwestern Australia in the later part of the nineteenth century. The man obtained the bottle glass from the typical olive-green ale bottle which was ubiquitous on the late nineteenth-century Australian frontier, perhaps picking it up from the town or mission bottle dump. It is possible that the spearhead was made on the spot for Clement, a European collector who was willing to pay immediately in cash, or to trade something which would have been useful to the man who made it, like a metal knife blade or steel axe. Clement collected this point along with a number of other items of Aboriginal manufacture which he subsequently shipped back to England and sold to the Pitt Rivers Museum, thus beginning a long and lucrative period of trading in Australian Aboriginal artefacts with museums throughout Europe. This Kimberley Point was catalogued, labelled and chosen for display. It is now a museum object, and it is unlikely to be sold.

Like all biographies, this one is necessarily partial. It would, for example, be possible to further explore the biographical life of the spearhead in the museum – where has it been stored and with what, how has it been displayed, who has looked at it and how has it figured in academic and popular culture since it was obtained? I'm sure I haven't been the first person to study it since it was purchased more than a century ago. Similarly, we could extend our gaze further into the past and explore the manufacture of the particular bottle which formed the raw material for the spearhead, and the trajectory it followed to reach the town dump from whence it was obtained.

Object biographies, like biographical writing more generally, can obviously take many forms and be structured in many different ways – and you will learn more about these as you go on with your study in subsequent chapters of this book. You will need to develop your skills of close description and analysis before you feel confident to begin to do this yourself. But I hope that by looking at this example of an object biography you now have a better sense of the usefulness of biography as a concept in dealing with material culture as source material, and understand the distinction which was discussed earlier between object-driven and object-centred approaches, as well as the ways in which they might be usefully combined. In this case, I have been able to utilise not only specific information about this particular object by way of the accession register linked to the sticker on the outside of the point (an object-centred approach), but also more general information about how similar objects were used within the societies in which they were made and traded (an object-driven approach).

Lives of violins

Fiona Richards

The final examples in this chapter return to objects that were created in Europe, to show how the methods of object biographies are applicable to all objects. This chapter opened with a scene set in London, populated by the objects associated with getting up in the morning and settling down to working on a computer. The next group of objects are definitely not everyday items but they should be familiar. Music is a significant strand of culture, investigated by archaeologists and anthropologists as well as musicologists. While music comes to life as something that is performed, the material culture of music might be said to centre on musical instruments.

Some musical instruments are so highly regarded that they have acquired almost celebrity status. In these cases, the historical circumstances of their production and use by performers might be well documented (in contrast to the lack of written sources for the maker of the Kimberley Point discussed above). In particular, stringed instruments made in Cremona in Italy during the seventeenth and eighteenth centuries are revered above all others. Renowned violin-making dynasties in Cremona include the Amati, Guadagnini, Guarneri and Tononi families. The most famous are the Stradivari family, and a Stradivarius, or Strad, is today one of the world's most sought-after violins (there are also some violas and cellos). Of this family, the best-known maker was Antonio Stradivari (1644–1737). Object biographies for this group of instruments could investigate the shared production techniques used in Cremona during these centuries, taking an object-driven approach to investigating why these instruments are still highly regarded.

Stradivarius violins (see, for instance, Figure 1.18) are renowned for their rich depth and individuality of sound. Each instrument was made by hand, and although the exact techniques of construction remain elusive, some aspects are known – for example, that a combination of spruce, willow and maple woods was used. Recent theories around the reasons for the quality of these instruments focus on the age and density of the wood used, and the nature of the varnish.

At a later stage in the object biography, these instruments have acquired exceptional economic value. A Strad made in the early 1700s can be worth huge sums of money: in 2011 a violin made in 1721 sold for £9.8 million. As each instrument is unique, the violins have acquired individual names, sometimes taken from their former players or owners. Some of these instruments have become museum objects, but, where this is so, they have entered institutions whose approach to representing material culture is quite different from the 'cultural evolution' mission of the early archaeology and anthropology galleries. Rather, the violins are collected as representations of exceptional human achievement, particularly excellence in the arts. While music-making is a theme that Pitt Rivers could have included in his collection of objects, notice how the Stradivarius instruments are held by museums that are primarily for works of art, understood as fine art (painting, drawing and sculpture) and decorative art (ceramics, textiles, glass and metalwork). The curators have made a judgement that the particular violins in their care have aesthetic qualities that are excellent and very rare, as examples of craft. These instruments can be displayed as single objects, as works of art, rather than placed at the end of a type series of stringed instruments played with a bow, as Pitt Rivers might have done.

While some of these instruments are used in performance today, others remain preserved in museum collections. The Ashmolean Museum, part of the University of Oxford, owns the 'Messiah' Strad, which is in immaculate condition as it has only rarely been played. Indeed, the violin was bequeathed to the museum with the express stipulation that it could not be played, but should be preserved as a means of studying craftsmanship. This instrument has been a showcase item for many

Figure 1.18 Violin by Antonio Stradivari, 1716. Photo: © Ashmolean Museum/Mary Evans

years, appearing in 1872 at an exhibition at the Kensington Museum (now the Victoria and Albert) and inspiring many articles and commentaries. During the Second World War it was moved to a country house for safekeeping, along with other items owned by the Ashmolean.

Other Stradivarius violins have had complicated and often mysterious lives, passed down from owner to owner, travelling the world. These violins can also be discussed in terms of an object-centred approach, using historical records of ownership and performance. A few examples serve to give you some idea of these violins' biographies:

- The 'Red Mendelssohn' (1721) inspired a 1988 film, *The Red Violin*.
- The 'Davidoff-Morini' (1727) was stolen from a New York apartment in 1995 and remains missing.
- The 'Gibson ex-Huberman' (1713) has a colourful history. At one time it was owned by Bronisław Huberman (1882–1947), a renowned Jewish violinist who in 1936 founded the Palestine Symphony Orchestra (now the Israel Philharmonic Orchestra). However, the violin was stolen twice during Huberman's lifetime. The first time it was soon returned; the second time it disappeared for 50 years but was then recovered following the confession of the thief. It subsequently passed into the hands of a member of the Amadeus Quartet, Norbert Brainin (1923–2005), who sold it to the American violinist Joshua Bell in 2001.

Activity

You can hear Bell playing the 'Gibson ex-Huberman' in the audio recording 'Joshua Bell playing Massenet', which you can find on the module website. Listen to this now before reading on.

Activity

Looking back at the ways in which Stradivarius violins have been treated over the years, what do you think are the contexts which you would need to know in order to write a longer object-driven biography of a violin? In contrast, what is the evidence for the 'celebrity' nature of object-centred biographies here?

You should allow about 20 minutes for this activity.

Discussion

I would need to understand more about the place of the violin in European music in order to ask questions about why makers of good violins became important and how they handed their craft on within a family. The materials used for violins do not seem to be inherently expensive, compared with gold or diamonds, so much of their original significance might come from the cultural values attached to the importance of making music with them. It is clear that the violins have acquired enormous economic value over time, and so an understanding of the economics of the specialist market that they can be traded in (the world's auction houses, for instance) might help in writing the latest stages of their biography as a group.

Individual violins have acquired their own names, and so I would expect them to have plenty of provenance information that could be used for an object-centred biography. Giving an object a name is a practice known from the Kula cycle, although the contexts in which these violins are exchanged are completely different – once a Strad has been paid for, the seller has no expectation of receiving one back! The violin that is now in a museum is at a very different stage in its biography compared with those that are still circulating and being played as part of a living tradition.

1.5 The life cycle of objects

In the same way that a person is born, lives and dies, going through a number of different rites of passage which mark the shift in context from one stage of life to the next, so objects might also be thought to undergo changes in context, to be born, to live and to die. For example, the life cycle of the Kimberley Points which ended up in museum collections include a significant moment when the points left the community that created them. A life cycle is a very broad description of the stages of life, and it is not necessarily very informative. Humans can be grouped on the basis of demographic factors, like place of birth, gender and lifestyle, to suggest general models of life cycles. For example, manual workers who smoke may leave school aged 16, work for 50 years, own 7 cars throughout their lifetime, have 2.7 children and die before the age of 73 (this is a fictional model). Similarly, the life cycle of plates sold by the Ikea chain store could begin with the mining of china clay and end with deposition in a landfill site after 16.2 years (to take a wild guess at the lifespan of plates). Similar patterns are observed in the data from large groups; your chain-smoking uncle and your own Ikea plate might have very different individual biographies, but put millions of examples together for analysis, and the life cycles emerge.

The idea of a life cycle for material culture is useful because it can tell us what happens, in general, to most objects of a particular type. Instead of trying to remember all the possible changes that could take place in an object's life, in order to research its biography, the life cycle provides a useful model for how to structure a biography. It is a way of grouping related stages in a life under broad headings: production, consumption and afterlife (see Figure 1.19).

We can look back at the objects introduced in this chapter to notice how their biographies used this three-part life-cycle structure. The first phase of the life cycle of objects involves their *production*: the procurement of raw materials, the design and manufacture of the object. This is like the 'birth' or 'gestation' and 'childhood' phases of an organic life-cycle model. The second stage of the life cycle of objects involves their *consumption* and use. We have tried to acknowledge several types of 'uses' here, including the immediate use of an item in terms of the function for which it was manufactured (a stone knife may be manufactured on the spot to butcher meat, for example), as well as processes of exchange and gift giving, which form another, secondary

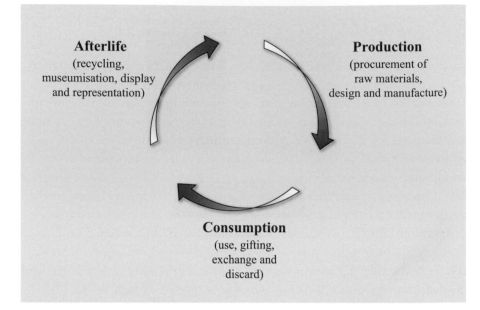

Figure 1.19   The life cycle of objects

type of 'use', or utility, as something going beyond the immediate function of the object (this is discussed further in Chapter 2). We saw examples of this type of use in relation to the Kula valuables and, exchanged in a market economy, Stradivarius violins when they become symbols of major investment as well as excellent musical instruments. This might be considered to equate to the 'adulthood' phase of a human life cycle.

Consumption

This is a term used within economics to mean how goods and services end up with their purchasers. Looking at my place in a wealthy, western society, I know I am a consumer of objects, or that I use objects to help me consume experiences. Consumption is the process by which individuals obtain goods and services, and in the present-day west it is dominated by economic transactions. However, here we are using 'consumption' as a broad term to cover how objects are acquired and used, and perhaps passed on. There may not be an economic transaction involved, or the object may not completely leave its producer. Consumption, then, is the 'in use' stage of an object's life. This broad definition does not determine what the use should be, and goes beyond economic value. My fondness for my chipped breakfast bowl, which was originally a gift, goes beyond its economic value. It is one of the objects that makes my house a home.

Finally, we have included an *afterlife* stage of the life cycle. This acknowledges the significant function which many objects have even after they have ceased to function or have become outdated. Think of the way in which some objects change their meaning and function by being removed from their original context of use and exhibited or re-staged in different cultural contexts. The objects we have been looking at from the Pitt Rivers Museum are a good example of this. While objects can become dormant, or 'die' and leave the cycle at any stage, they can also sometimes be reanimated and gain new meanings, re-entering the cycle at a later date. The Stradivarius violins now in museum collections are dormant as performance instruments (if they are not allowed to be played), but they have a celebrity which endures with the appreciation of the craft and performance that they exemplify.

Activity

Take any *type* of object which you can think of – perhaps something which is in front of you on your desk or table, or wherever you are as you read this chapter – and try to apply this life-cycle model to it. Don't worry too much about the detail, but perhaps think about some of the ways in which the meaning of this type of object changes as such objects shift through different stages of their life and appear in different contexts and places. To help you, you could jot down the headings used in the example given above.

You should allow about 15 minutes for this activity.

Now think about the biography of that *particular* object. In what ways do you think the object biography of that specific item differs from the generic life cycle which might be expected for other such items? In what way does this illustrate the difference between an object biography and the life cycle of objects?

Discussion

I hope you found applying the life-cycle model to an object of your choice helpful in organising your thoughts about the biographies of objects. You might, for example, have chosen a pen which you picked up from your desk. While that individual pen has a *biography* which links it to you directly (you might, for instance, have written about how you purchased it yesterday because you realised you needed it for your studies), we can only generalise about the *life cycle* of pens more broadly, based on the shared experiences of many other pens used by many other people – their production, marketing and purchase, and our general knowledge about their use.

Research in the humanities needs different tools according to the questions to be answered. If you think back to the possible life cycle for a human suggested at the start of this section, based on demographic factors, you may realise that the life-cycle model is useful for making predictions. It is valuable for public health policy, for instance. Similarly, life-cycle models for mass-produced household objects might be essential for insurance companies or environmental waste policymakers, although it has to be said they are of less interest to the questions that the humanities ask about the meaning of human culture. Object biographies use the life-cycle model to structure their narratives about how objects carry, make and shift in meaning. Like reading a good story, the life-cycle model reminds us to ask, 'What happened next?' The interesting answers come with the detail of the object biography.

Conclusion

This chapter has covered a lot of ground – both conceptually and geographically. We have followed the passage of objects from former colonies into the museums of Britain and North America, and moved from the museum to the field and back again. In doing so, we have explored the genesis of 'material culture' as an area of academic study in the development of modes of classifying and ordering objects which were obtained from different cultures, and in the foundation of the disciplines of Archaeology and Anthropology in the late nineteenth century. We looked in detail at the case study of the Kula cycle, which was studied by Malinowski as part of the shift away from the focus on objects in Anthropology and the development of Archaeology as a separate discipline, and which helped suggest a number of ways in which objects might be thought to have biographies, and even 'social lives'. Drawing on these ideas, we have considered the idea of object biographies and the life cycles of objects, ideas to which we shall return in a number of places in this book.

References

Appadurai, A. (1986) 'Introduction: commodities and the politics of value', in Appadurai, A. (ed.) *The Social Life of Things: Commodities in Cultural Perspective*, Cambridge, Cambridge University Press, pp. 3–63.

Bennett, T. (2004) *Pasts beyond Memory: Evolution, Museums, Colonialism*, London and New York, Routledge.

Boas, F. (1887) 'Museums of ethnology and their classification', *Science*, vol. 9, no. 228, pp. 587–9.

Boas, F. (1940) *Race, Language and Culture*, New York, The Company.

Buchli, V. (2002) 'Introduction', in Buchli, V. (ed.) *The Material Culture Reader*, Oxford and New York, Berg, pp. 1–22.

Clement, E. (1904) 'Ethnographical notes on the Western Australian Aborigines (with a descriptive catalogue of a collection of ethnographical objects from Western Australia by J.D.E. Schmeltz)', *Internationales Archiv für Ethnographie*, vol. 16, nos. 1–2, pp. 1–27.

Conn, S. (1998) *Museums and American Intellectual Life, 1876–1926*, Chicago, University of Chicago Press.

Gosden, C. and Larson, F. (2007) *Knowing Things: Exploring the Collections at the Pitt Rivers Museum 1884–1945*, Oxford, Oxford University Press.

Harrison, R. (2006) 'An artefact of colonial desire: Kimberley Points and the technologies of enchantment', *Current Anthropology*, vol. 47, no. 1, pp. 63–88.

Harrison, R. (2010) 'Stone tools', in Hicks, D. and Beaudry, M. (eds) *The Oxford Handbook of Material Culture Studies*, Oxford and New York, Oxford University Press, pp. 515–36.

Hoskins, J.A. (1998) *Biographical Objects: How Things Tell the Stories of People's Lives*, London and New York, Routledge.

Hoskins, J.A. (2006) 'Agency, objects and biography', in Tilley, C., Keane, W., Kuechler, S., Rowlands, M. and Spyer, P. (eds) *Sage Handbook of Material Culture*, London and New York, Sage, pp. 74–85.

Jacknis, I. (1985) 'Franz Boas and exhibits: on the limitations of the museum method of anthropology', in Stocking, G.W. (ed.) *Objects and Others: Essays on Museums and Material Culture*, Madison, WI, University of Wisconsin Press, pp. 75–111.

Kopytoff, I. (1986) 'The cultural biography of things: commoditization as process', in Appadurai, A. (ed.) *The Social Life of Things: Commodities in Cultural Perspective*, Cambridge, Cambridge University Press, pp. 64–91.

Leach, J. and Leach, E. (1983) *The Kula: New Perspectives on Massim Exchange*, Cambridge and New York, Cambridge University Press.

Loftus, D. and Wood, P. (2008) 'The art of Benin: changing relations between Europe and Africa II', in Danson Brown, R. (ed.) *Cultural Encounters* (AA100 Book1), Milton Keynes, The Open University, pp. 43–88.

Malinowski, B. (1922) *Argonauts of the Western Pacific: An Account of Native Enterprise and Adventure in the Archipelagoes of Melanesian New Guinea*, London, George Routledge & Sons.

Oxford English Dictionary (2010) [Online], Oxford, Oxford University Press. Available at http://www.oed.com (Accessed 19 March 2014).

Pitt Rivers, A.H.L.F. (1875) 'On the evolution of culture', *Proceedings of the Royal Anthropological Institute*, vol. 7, pp. 496–520.

Pitt Rivers, A.H.L.F. (1906) *The Evolution of Culture and Other Essays* (ed. J.L. Myers, intro. H. Balfour), Oxford, Clarendon Press.

Trigger, B. (1996) *A History of Archaeological Thought*, London and New York, Routledge.

Further reading

Talal Asad (1973) has edited a collection of essays which were published at a time when anthropologists were actively investigating the history of their discipline and its relationship with the processes of colonialism. These essays explore how anthropologists were enabled by colonial administration to undertake fieldwork and debate the impact on indigenous societies. Chris Gosden and Yvonne Marshall (1999) provide an introduction to a collection of articles in one volume of a journal; they discuss recent thinking by anthropologists about object biographies, making use of the Pitt Rivers collection along with other examples. Harold Mytum is an archaeologist, who has written (2003/4) about analysing gravestones as objects rather than as stones with historical text carved on them. His research is an example of object biographies for historical, western archaeology.

Asad, T. (ed.) (1973) *Anthropology and the Colonial Encounter*, London, Ithaca Press.

Gosden, C. and Marshall, Y. (1999) 'The cultural biography of objects', *World Archaeology*, vol. 31, no. 2, pp. 169–78 [Online]. Available at http://www.jstor.org.libezproxy.open.ac.uk/stable/125055 (Accessed 24 October 2013).

Mytum, H. (2003/4) 'Artefact biography as an approach to material culture: Irish gravestones as a material form of genealogy', *Journal of Irish Archaeology*, vols 12/13, pp. 111–27 [Online]. Available at http://www.jstor.org.libezproxy.open.ac.uk/stable/20650834 (Accessed 24 October 2013).

Chapter 2
Classifying and describing objects

Phil Perkins and Jessica Hughes with Fiona Richards

Contents

Aims

This chapter will:

- encourage you to identify and analyse the categorisation of sounds and objects

- enable you to practise and develop your skills of observation and description of objects

- enable you to interpret objects and work towards writing your own object life cycles

- introduce you to case studies on music databases, an object in the British Museum, and the life cycle and ways of classifying Athenian vases.

Materials you will need

In this chapter, you will need to listen to the following audio recordings, which can be found on the module website:

- Coltrane, 'My favorite things'
- Tabor, 'He fades away'
- Merce, 'Del amanecer'
- Bartoli, 'Son qual nave'
- Pet Shop Boys, 'It's a sin'
- Mercury and Caballé, 'Barcelona'.

You will also be directed to the website in order to access an online sound database and the online database of the collections of the British Museum.

Introduction

This chapter concentrates on describing and classifying objects. You will be considering ways in which various types of material are categorised, as well as reading and writing descriptions and considering why descriptions are important. Throughout the chapter you will be exploring how things and words written about things are inextricably linked, and the issues involved with classification. You will be working with a range of objects drawn from different times and different parts of the world. Some of these you might expect to meet in Art History; others in Classical Studies, History or Music: they are brought together to be studied here so that you can practise applying the same study techniques to a diverse range of artefacts.

In the first chapter of this book, you studied the Kula cycle: there the emphasis was on the 'social life' of objects and the objects were interpreted with reference to social practices observed in a living society. In this chapter, we shall focus on the classification of things, a topic that you have already met in your work on early anthropological museums. In Chapter 1, you were introduced to the ideas of a small group of nineteenth-century scholars (including Christian Jürgensen Thomsen and Augustus Henry Lane Fox Pitt Rivers) who each chose to classify material culture according to a chronological and evolutionary sequence. As you discovered, not only did these classifications reflect contemporary scientific beliefs but they were also influenced by tacit and now discredited cultural beliefs about the primacy of Europe within world history. Your work in Chapter 1, then, has already indicated that the ordering principles imposed by us on objects are never neutral, but can always tell us something about the assumptions and preoccupations of the people who invented them.

In the first section of this chapter you will study the classification of music, a subject which may seem familiar and straightforward, but actually involves a myriad options. You will consider different approaches to classification and use databases to explore their efficacy.

You will return to databases in the second section of the chapter, which moves from the familiar (music) to the unfamiliar. Here you will focus on an object in isolation from its society and work on developing the meaning of an unfamiliar object through the use of description. The third section of the chapter will further develop your work on the classification of objects in relation to a case study drawn from classical archaeology: Athenian vases from the sixth and fifth centuries BCE. It has been estimated that as many as 200,000 Athenian vases survive – even so, this is a very small percentage of what once was. How have scholars made sense of this great mass of material?

This chapter consolidates your understanding of the methods of using the model of an object life cycle (production, consumption and afterlife) to structure an object biography. The case studies in this chapter are object-centred, in that they prioritise the history of some individual objects, without excluding the need to understand the group they belong to.

2.1 Classifying music

DICK: I guess it looks as if you're reorganising your records? Um, what is this? Chronological?

ROB: Nope.

DICK: Not alphabetical?

ROB: Nope.

DICK: What?

ROB: Autobiographical.

DICK: No … way?!

ROB: Yep. I can tell you how I got from Deep Purple to Howlin' Wolf in just twenty-five moves. And if I want to find the song 'Landslide' by Fleetwood Mac, I have to remember that I bought it for someone in the 'Fall of 1983' pile. But didn't give it to them for personal reasons.

DICK: That sounds …

ROB: Comforting.

(High Fidelity, 2000)

If you've seen the film *High Fidelity* (see Figure 2.1), which is based on the Nick Hornby novel of the same name, you may well recognise this dialogue between two of the film's central characters – Rob, the Chicago record-store owner whose own back-catalogue of romantic relationships is the film's main subject, and Dick, his unpaid store assistant. In the scene quoted above, Dick has called round to Rob's flat to find his shelves empty and the floor strewn with tall piles of records. This is the 'reorganising' familiar to many a music fanatic, motivated in this instance by the departure of Rob's long-term girlfriend. Rob has devised a typology for his collection, although one that is not immediately obvious to anyone else.

This dialogue encapsulates some important points about classifying things. First of all, and most simply, it shows the pervasiveness of classifications in our everyday lives. Although typologies were

Figure 2.1 Still image from the film *High Fidelity* (2000), directed by Stephen Frears, released by Touchstone Pictures. Photo: Melissa Moseley/Album/akg-images

introduced in Chapter 1 as an academic method, they are not the unique preserve of the archaeologist or museum curator. They are all around us in the home and the workplace. Second, the exchange reminds us that most collections of things can be ordered in many different ways, each of which reflects a particular value-system. There is no single, self-evident way of classifying Rob's immense record collection: chronological, alphabetical and autobiographical methods are all mentioned here, but there are many more possible categories and sub-categories that might have been used.

This particular example of Rob's record collection is particularly pertinent, as music is a subject that lends itself to classification in many different ways. It might be ordered by genre in the broadest sense, for example folk, pop, rock, classical. Or a composer's output might be sorted by type, such as vocal and instrumental.

Classifying music by sound

Fiona Richards

One way in which music can be classified is by sound production. When Pitt Rivers donated his large collection of objects to the University of Oxford, it included 300 musical instruments, and these were organised according to their characteristics. By 1939 the musical instrument collection numbered over 4000 items, with many new groups of instruments added to the collection over the next 30 years, including barrel organs and mechanical musical instruments. The steady increase in the number of instruments held by the museum has meant that some system of ordering them is essential.

One traditional method of doing so, known as the Sachs-Hornbostel system and dating back to an ancient Sanskrit text, the *Natya Shastra*, divides instruments into four main groups as follows:

- idiophones, which produce sound by vibrating themselves
- membranophones, which produce sound by a vibrating membrane
- chordophones, which produce sound by vibrating strings
- aerophones, which produce sound by vibrating columns of air.

A perhaps more familiar way of classifying musical instruments, especially within the western classical tradition, is to divide them into families, again according to the ways in which their sound is produced – those that are bowed or plucked (strings), those that are blown (wind) or struck (percussion), and keyboard instruments. To give more detail:

- Bowed instruments – such as the violin, viola, cello and double bass – are played primarily by pulling a bow across the strings, although they can also be plucked to a limited degree.
- Plucked instruments – such as the guitar – produce sound exclusively by the action of plucking or strumming the strings.
- Wind instruments can be split into two separate categories: woodwind and brass – literally because one group is made of wood, the other of brass. The flute is an exception to this. Originally a wooden instrument, it is now made from silver, gold or platinum.
- Instruments that produce sound by being struck are generally referred to as percussion instruments. However, this definition covers a vast array of instruments, so they are normally divided into two categories: those of 'indefinite pitch' (which are not tuned to a pitch, for example

2.2 Looking at, describing and identifying objects

In the previous section, the excerpt of dialogue from the film *High Fidelity* (2000) raised the problem of how methods of classification are not necessarily shared by everyone. The classification of music, whether by instrument, genre or performance, is also driven by the question of why the classification needs to be made: is it, for instance, to store and retrieve instruments or to promote the sale of recordings? In this section, we shall follow up these problems of classification systems that are able to be widely shared and examine the uses of classification.

First, you should read the following comic poem about meeting an object:

The Blind Men and the Elephant

I

It was six men of Indostan
To learning much inclined,
Who went to see the Elephant
(Though all of them were blind),
That each by observation
Might satisfy his mind.

II

The *First* approached the Elephant,
And happening to fall
Against his broad and sturdy side,
At once began to bawl:
'God bless me! – but the Elephant
Is very like a wall!'

III

The *Second*, feeling of the tusk,
Cried: 'Ho! – what have we here
So very round and smooth and sharp?
To me 'tis mighty clear
This wonder of an Elephant
Is very like a spear!'

IV

The *Third* approached the animal,
And happening to take
The squirming trunk within his hands,

Thus boldly up and spake:
'I see,' quoth he, 'the Elephant
Is very like a snake!'

V

The *Fourth* reached out his eager hand,
And felt about the knee.
'What most this wondrous beast is like
Is mighty plain,' quoth he;
''Tis clear enough the Elephant
Is very like a tree!'

VI

The *Fifth*, who chanced to touch the ear,
Said: 'E'en the blindest man
Can tell what this resembles most;
Deny the fact who can,
This marvel of an Elephant
Is very like a fan!'

VII

The *Sixth* no sooner had begun
About the beast to grope,
Than, seizing on the swinging tail
That fell within his scope,
'I see,' quoth he, 'the Elephant
Is very like a rope!'

VIII

And so these men of Indostan
Disputed loud and long,
Each in his own opinion
Exceeding stiff and strong,
Though each was partly in the right,
And all were in the wrong!

MORAL

So, oft in theologic wars
The disputants, I ween,
Rail on in utter ignorance
Of what each other mean,
And prate about an Elephant
Not one of them has seen!

(Saxe, 1873, pp. 77–8)

This poem pinpoints a set of challenges faced by everyone meeting an object for the first time. The central verses each use the same structure to carry their narrative. A man meets an elephant, makes an observation using his senses ('happening to fall/Against his broad and sturdy side'), tries to understand his observation by interpreting it in terms of his previously acquired knowledge ('the Elephant/Is very like a wall!') and then communicates his interpretation. Now it's your turn to use these same three stages: observation, interpretation and communication.

Activity

You should allow about 10 minutes for this activity.

Look at Figure 2.2. It shows four sides of an object. This is probably the first time you have met this object. In order to answer the questions below, you will need to:

* observe the object in the photographs (the caption provides a little information to help)
* interpret your observation
* communicate your observation.

Now answer the following questions:

1   How big is the object?
2   What is the object made of?
3   What shape is the object?
4   How was the object made?
5   What colour is the object?

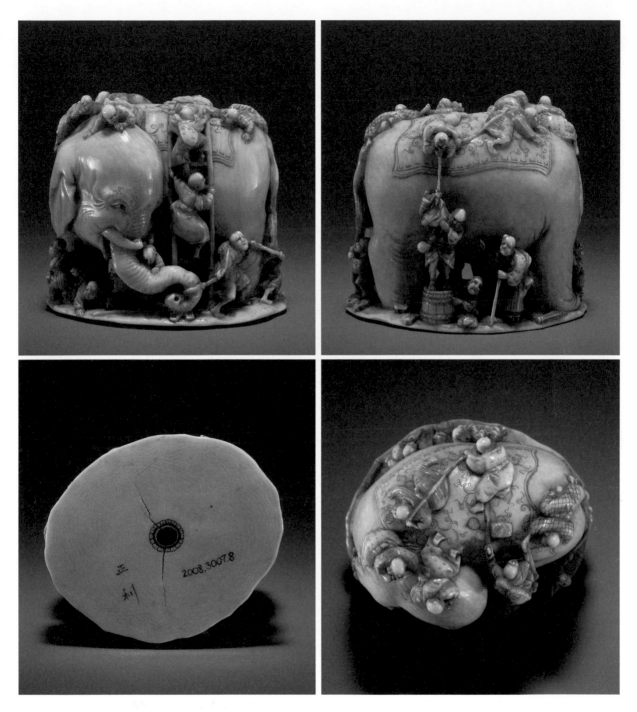

Figure 2.2 An object from the British Museum, ivory, length 4.7cm, depth 4cm. British Museum, London, 2008,3007.8. Photo: © The Trustees of the British Museum

Discussion

1   The caption helps: the object is 4.7cm long and 4cm deep. We might estimate it is 5cm high.

2   The caption tells us it is ivory, but without that information we would struggle to say something like 'a light-coloured, brownish-yellow substance with a reflective surface'. We might guess it to be ivory, but it could easily be stone or plastic. Even if we had guessed it is ivory, what kind of ivory is it? Is it elephant, mammoth, hippopotamus or walrus ivory? Only very detailed observation could tell us this. Perhaps an expert with a lens or a scientific analysis could provide an answer.

3   The base is oval or nearly circular, the sides vertical and the top domed, although the surfaces are shaped further by the carving. The observation of this overall shape is consistent with the identification as ivory because the shape is generally that of a piece of tusk, possibly the pointed end, the material from which the object was fashioned.

4   There are few visible clues as to how this object was made. Presumably the object was carved, but there are no obvious tool marks. The details of the design are very finely cut into the surface: the wrinkles around the elephant's eye and tusk have been very carefully cut with a fine, sharp tool. Some of the details (the elephant's eyebrows and the ground, for example) have been dotted in, presumably with the aid of a sharp tool. The hole in the underside was presumably drilled with a fine tool.

5   The object has a variable colour. It is mostly brownish yellow, but the cut decoration is generally darker. Perhaps a coloured substance has been rubbed into the cut surface, but the darker areas could just be accumulated grime.

It is worth remembering that you have been looking at photographs. If you had been able to hold the object in your hand, you would have had an immediate impression of its size (rather than having to get this information from the caption). By using your sense of touch you would have been able to make more observations – about the object's weight and texture, for example. While holding it, you could have rotated the object to understand it in three dimensions, looked underneath it, examined the material (ivory) from which it has been crafted. With a magnifying glass, you could have seen more detail and been able to observe aspects of the object not visible to the naked eye.

Any observation of any object will always be limited in some way. Perhaps the object is dimly lit, or behind glass, or perhaps touching it is prohibited. Or, as in this case, perhaps you are seeing only a representation of the object. Nevertheless, our brains subconsciously do a lot of work on our behalf and help us to understand what we see in an image of an object as if it were a real object in front of us. Some aspects are difficult to grasp from a photograph, particularly a sense of scale (this object is only 4.7cm long) and an accurate perception of colour. So, all in all, any description based on photographs will never be able to capture all aspects of an object.

If observations are limited by various factors, then our ability to interpret what we observe is also limited by our previous knowledge or our ability to work out what we are looking at. With the object you have been studying, you might have observed the shape and details making up the various parts of an elephant. You probably also observed and recognised the ladder and the human figures. Some of the smaller parts are more difficult to observe and identify. As in the poem by Saxe, your interpretations are shaped by what you can observe.

This kind of observation (close looking) produces the raw material for the first stages of reconstructing an object's biography, structured through the life-cycle model (production, consumption and afterlife). By piecing together observations and assumptions about what has been observed, it is possible to outline the production of the object.

Activity

Combine what you have observed about the object in Figure 2.2 and the discussion in the activity above to write a brief account of the earliest stage of this object's biography – its production.

You should allow about 10 minutes for this activity.

Discussion

Despite the lack of certainty around some of the observations, it is possible to outline a basic sequence of events. Here is my attempt:

Somewhere in Africa or India an elephant grew a tusk (assuming the object is made of elephant ivory). The elephant died and its tusk was removed and taken to a workshop. A small piece, possibly the end of the tusk, was cut off. This was intricately carved to create a small (4–4.7cm) object in the shape of an elephant with a blanket on its back. The elephant is standing upright with its head turned back and lowered. A ladder runs up one flank of the elephant and a rope dangles down the other. Numerous small figures crawl over and around the elephant, some climbing up or down from the elephant's back. The figures were created by carving into the ivory, cutting out the figures in high relief. The surface was smoothed and polished. Details such as faces, wrinkles and clothes were carved into the surface with a fine tool. These details may have been coloured by the application of a dark brown substance. A hole was drilled on the underside and further decoration added to the otherwise flat underside.

At this point it is possible to identify the end of the production process of the object. The object might then be said to be 'finished' and ready for use, or consumption – the next stage of its biography.

Activity

Look again at the object in Figure 2.2. Are there any features of the object that you think might be related to its use? Is there any evidence of damage or wear on the surfaces?

Discussion

There is not much to go on. The object is small – it could fit into a hand. It is intricately decorated, suggesting that it was intended to be seen, and perhaps used, in a place where it could be closely inspected and admired. The hole in the centre of the underside is unexplained. It is not apparent how deep the hole is or if it goes right through the object. There are two cracks to either side of the hole, which may suggest that the object is old, or that it has been exposed to variable humidity and the consequent expansion and contraction have caused it to crack. There does not seem to be significant wear around the edge of the hole. On the upper side, all of the protruding parts – the heads of the human figures especially – seem very smooth and highly polished. They are a lighter colour and very shiny. This may be the result of rubbing or constant handling of the object. This suggests that the object may have had an active life, although there are no signs of damage such as missing heads.

Overall, there is little evidence to enable us to identify the function of the object. From the evidence we have it is difficult to answer the questions 'What was it for?' or 'What did it do?'

At this point we have reached the limits of what can be achieved by observing the object alone. We need to use our own prior knowledge, or, failing that, ask someone else or consult a reference source that might be able to identify the object.

Activity

Do you know, or think you know, what the object is? If so, write down the reasons you think you know what it is. If you don't know what it is, go straight on to the discussion.

Discussion

If you know what the object is, what is it that gave you that understanding? Is it something specific, like the size, shape or material? Or is it a combination of characteristics, like the size, shape *and* material together? Or did you just know what it is because you have seen something like it before? It is often difficult to pinpoint why you recognise something as 'similar', but this probably involves some very general features such as size, shape and material, and perhaps some details about the way an object has been shaped or decorated.

Obviously enough, our mystery object doesn't look like an everyday object you might find at home or at work. So another approach to identifying the object could be to take it to a museum and ask an expert curator to identify it. In the twenty-first century we can also use the internet to help identify objects. However, using a search engine would be even less helpful than wandering around a large museum hoping to spot something similar (searching Google for 'ivory object' images yields hundreds of thousands of results). A more academic approach is to search the collections of a museum that are available online: these can be used like reference works.

Databases

This module makes use of databases, particularly those created for collections of objects. Collections databases can be thought of as a gathering together of all the descriptions of objects in a museum in such a way that they can be searched for information or organised in different ways.

For databases to work, or for any comparisons of objects to be made, it is necessary to have some degree of standardisation in descriptions of objects. Just like any filing system or address book, big museum databases need a highly standardised structure and use of vocabulary. They won't work well if, for example, the material that some objects are made of is described as 'ivory' while for others it is described as 'elephant tusk'. The amount of detail that needs to be recorded and the structure of standardised descriptions will vary according to the reasons why the objects are being described, but a minimum necessary to communicate a basic range of information about an object would be:

- what the object is (identification)
- what it is made of
- where it was made
- when it was made
- where it was found
- where it is now
- its dimensions
- a unique number to distinguish it from other similar items.

Other items of information might also be useful, such as information about who owns the object, its completeness or its physical condition.

Activity

You should allow about 30 minutes for this activity and the next two.

For this activity, you will need to look at the online database of the collections of the British Museum. You can do this by following the link provided on the module website.

Once you are on the British Museum website, you should search the collections database by typing 'ivory elephant' into the search box. Click on the option for 'images only' and start the search. Then examine the first page of results. Are there any objects similar to our mystery object?

Discussion

At the time of writing this search produced 199 objects. The first page of results included an image resembling our object. It is only generally similar – a roughly carved and somewhat hairy elephant, described as a 'toy; gaming-piece; figure' from the Roman period. This description could conceivably apply to our object, but it is not very precise. We need to find a more similar object.

Activity

Now return to the online database of the collections of the British Museum and this time type 'ivory elephant men' into the search box. Click on the option for 'images only' and, again, start the search.

Examine the first page of results. Are there any images similar to our mystery object? This page should include a small picture of a familiar item. Click on the image and you will be shown all of the information the museum keeps on record about the object.

Discussion

At the time of writing, under the heading 'Description', it read: 'Netsuke. Blind men climbing over an elephant. Made of ivory.' This is a description written by the museum staff. It is very brief – especially when compared with the detail that we have been discussing. It also does not appear to be an account that is based purely on observation. Is it possible to identify the men in the object as 'blind'? Also, what does 'netsuke' mean?

This sort of description is an identification. Now you know what this object is called, you could use the identification to go on and search for more information. A netsuke (pronounced 'netski') is a small toggle used to attach a cord to the belt of a Japanese kimono. Items such as boxes or pouches could then be suspended from the cord.

Activity

Go back to the information about our netsuke on the British Museum collections database. Look at the categories of information presented about the netsuke and decide whether they are based on observation or on prior knowledge. If the information is based on prior knowledge, think about how this might have been acquired.

Jot down your findings in the form of a table. On the left, list each category of information; in the middle, note whether you think observation or prior knowledge (or both) is involved here; on the right, note the probable source of the information (if this applies).

Discussion

Table 2.1 sets out my thoughts on what is presented on the web page of the museum's database.

Table 2.1   Categories of information for the British Museum's netsuke

Category	Observation or prior knowledge	Probable source
Object types	Prior knowledge	Learning or reading about Japanese objects
Museum number	Observation and prior knowledge	It is written on the base
Description	Observation and prior knowledge	There is some observation, but 'blind' and 'netsuke' are prior knowledge
Date	Prior knowledge	Learning or reading or possibly scientific techniques such as radiocarbon dating
Production place	Prior knowledge	Don't know; perhaps they are commonly found or still manufactured in Japan. Perhaps their specialised use on a kimono is relevant only in Japan
Materials	Observation	
Technique	Observation	Although some knowledge is also required. (Technique is a term used in museums to mean 'which techniques were used in the manufacture of the object')
Dimensions	Observation	
Inscription type	Observation and prior knowledge	Need to have learned to read Japanese
Inscription transliteration	Observation and prior knowledge	Need to have learned to read the Japanese alphabet
Exhibition history	Prior knowledge	Museum records of exhibitions
Conservation	Prior knowledge	Museum records of conservation treatments
Subjects	Observation	
Acquisition name	Prior knowledge	Records will have been kept about the object when it was acquired by the museum

Acquisition date	Observation and prior knowledge	The date of acquisition has been written in ink on the bottom of the netsuke and records will have been kept about the object when it was acquired by the museum
Acquisition notes	Prior knowledge	Information provided by previous owners
Department	Prior knowledge	
Registration number	Observation and prior knowledge	

Some of my ideas about the sources of prior knowledge are guesswork, but the museum will no doubt have more detailed information that is not made public and some of the curators may have witnessed the object's arrival in the museum.

An identification

From your work on the collections database of the British Museum, you will have correctly identified the object. Further research in the museum and elsewhere could doubtless reveal more information about it. For example, the British Museum's *Report and Accounts* notes the arrival of related objects in the 12 months to March 2009:

> Japan featured prominently in the year's acquisitions. A fine impression of Hokusai's celebrated The Great Wave (1830–3) was acquired with support from The Art Fund. A group of 19th-century *netsuke*, accepted by HM Government in lieu of inheritance tax, was allocated to the [museum]. The 26 tiny carvings of ivory, horn or wood depict priests and devils, old women and babies, wolves and toads, and even two apes playing Go.
>
> (British Museum, 2009, p. 5)

Associated events had been reported in the *Daily Telegraph* on 14 November 2005:

Royal heirlooms for sale to pay death duties

Death duties, often regarded as the curse of the middle classes, have hit the Royal Family.

Prince Richard, Duke of Gloucester, a cousin of the Queen, announced yesterday that he is having to sell a large selection of property to pay the inheritance tax bill on the estate of his father, Prince Henry, Duke of Gloucester. In what is tantamount to a Royal Household clearance sale, Christie's will auction family heirlooms in January with prices ranging from £50 to more than £100,000.

The old duke's backgammon set, his collection of sporrans and his ancient cine-camera may tempt souvenir hunters. Serious collectors will be more interested in Prince Henry's rare books and paintings.

Prince Henry, the youngest brother of Edward VIII, who abdicated in 1936, and George VI, died in 1974, but the Inland Revenue deferred death duties until after the death of his widow, Princess Alice.

She died, the oldest royal in history, last October, aged 102. Their son, the present Duke of Gloucester, is hoping to raise £1 million from the sale.

(Daily Telegraph, 2005)

The information held by the museum helps reconstruct the 'consumption' stage of the netsuke's biography. It was probably given as a 'ritual gift' by the then emperor of Japan, Hirohito (1901–1989), to the Duke of Gloucester when the duke made a state visit to Japan in 1929 to confer the Order of the Garter on the emperor (Best, 2005; and see Figure 2.3). The visit was designed to improve Anglo-Japanese relations, and amid much exchange of ceremonial awards it seems likely that the netsuke was a gift rather than a private purchase. In these circumstances the netsuke was acting in a ceremonial role as a prestige gift rather than simply being an ordinary present of a belt toggle. Essentially, the netsuke was functioning in an imperial version of the Kula cycle (discussed in Chapter 1). Subsequently, the netsuke was transported around the world and became part of the collection of the Duke of Gloucester. The collection of 777 items referred to in the article above was sold at Christie's auction house in London in 2006 after some objects, including the netsuke, had been used to pay inheritance tax.

Figure 2.3 Emperor Hirohito being decorated with the Order of the Garter by the Duke of Gloucester, 1 June 1929. Photo: Gamma-Keystone via Getty Images

All these events relate to the biography of the netsuke as part of its transition from the phase of 'consumption' to the 'afterlife' stage in the object life cycle (see Chapter 1, Figure 1.19) as it underwent the process of 'museumisation'. In this case the UK government accepted ownership of the netsuke items in lieu of inheritance tax and passed them into the care of the British Museum. Once in the museum, the objects were catalogued: each was given a unique accession number and described, and all known details were recorded in the museum's catalogue of accessions.

The museum database shows subsequent events in the netsuke's life. It was lightly cleaned on 24 June 2009, displayed to the public from 1 July to 25 October that year as part of the exhibition 'Japan from prehistory to the present' at the British Museum, and then displayed again from October 2010 to 14 February 2011 in the same exhibition. Thousands of people must have seen it: a striking contrast to the time it was owned by Prince Henry, Duke of Gloucester, when there is no record of it being seen by anyone.

As the netsuke has moved through time it has changed location, visibility and ownership; it has also changed both its function (what it does or is) and its utility (what it is used for). The difference between the function of an object and its utility is subtle and reflects the difference between an object-centred approach and an object-driven approach. Essentially this is the difference between what an object was for (or what it was designed to do) and what it was actually used for by people (or what the artefact actually did itself).

Activity

You should allow about 15 minutes for this activity and the next one.

First of all, make a list of the various functions that our object has performed over its lifetime.

Discussion

Here's my list, and I'll try to surprise you with my starting point. The object has functioned as:

1   a tusk for digging, etc. (while still raw material)
2   a netsuke – a toggle on a kimono belt, for suspending objects
3   a chattel – an object with a monetary value
4   a museum object.

This varied list illustrates the changing functions that the same object may perform at different points in time.

Activity

Now make a list of the ways in which the netsuke was actually used during its lifetime.

Discussion

Here's my list. It has been used:

1 To display wealth as a precious object made from a precious raw material – in contrast to an elephant's digging tool.

2 To display the skill of an artisan/artist.

3 To attach a cord to a belt. That is to say, it may have been used as a netsuke – given the worn surface we have observed – in the period between the mid nineteenth century (when it was made) and 1929. Here its function and use actually coincide.

4 To exchange as a gift. It was probably given as a diplomatic gift and considered as suitable for this purpose because it was a prestigious object and a work of art.

5 To pay a debt as a proxy for money (a commodity exchange took place when it was used to pay taxes).

6 To exemplify Japanese art and artisanship in a museum in London, and also to play a part in all the other roles that museum objects perform in terms of education, culture and entertainment.

7 To help you learn about material culture!

All of these observations that we have made about the netsuke could contribute to its object biography. Some parts of the biography are well documented, while others are derived from an interpretation of what we can see and deduce from the object itself. We have been focusing much more on object-centred approaches to the netsuke, but it would be possible to look further into object-driven approaches and find out more about the makers, users, consumers or viewers of the object. We have already encountered some of the raw materials for an object-driven approach. For example, the **inscription** in Japanese characters on the base identifies the maker of the netsuke as Masanori; we could investigate him further and find other artefacts he made. We have encountered Emperor Hirohito and Prince Henry of Gloucester as users or consumers of the netsuke. What motivated them to become engaged with the artefact? Presumably the answer lies in its prestige value or aesthetic qualities. We could visit the British Museum to see it ourselves, or to observe other people encountering it and see what effect it has on them.

A final question to ask before moving on from the netsuke is, 'Does it have a meaning?' This takes us beyond just studying its function and use. A more focused question to start from is, 'What does the form of the netsuke represent?' The answer is straightforward enough: it is the same story told in the comic verse by John Godfrey Saxe, 'The Blind Men and the Elephant'. Yet the story is not Saxe's creation; it has ancient precedents in several non-European religions, appearing in the Buddhist scripture *Udana* and also later in Sufi Muslim and Hindu mysticism. Saxe's poem doesn't *explain* the figures on the netsuke – it is a separate representation of the same story that inspired the carving of the netsuke. They differ in their details and emphasis: the poem reflects the arguments between the men, whereas the netsuke shows the activity of the crawling men. The poem helps to interpret the netsuke because it is a version of the same story that the netsuke represents. In these eastern religious traditions the story is taken to symbolise the idea that things may be looked at from different points of view, or that partial information leads to argument and dissent. If the netsuke also carries these ideas through its life cycle, this may add another dimension to its social life: perhaps the netsuke might be interpreted as symbolising a concept appropriate to a diplomatic gift given as Britain and Japan attempted to find common ground in their approach to China in the 1920s. It was certainly chosen to be studied in this module because it symbolises different ways of looking at the same problem.

Meanings such as this only become apparent if an object can be situated in a cultural context, as, for example, in Japan where Buddhism is one of the major religions. Without knowledge of the story of the blind men and the elephant, the netsuke could be interpreted as simply representing an elephant with men crawling over it, so missing the association with relative points of view and disputes. This is an example of the cultural relativism developed from the ideas of Boas that you encountered in Chapter 1 – things may appear different from varying points of view.

Subjectivity and objectivity

This brings us to another important distinction that can be made between descriptions of objects. When describing an object, ask yourself, 'Am I being **subjective** or am I being **objective**?' The *Concise Oxford Dictionary of Archaeology* expresses the difference between the two terms when it defines objectivity as:

> The idea that things exist, or that statements about things are true, in absolute terms and independently of human existence or belief. Such a view stands in opposition to subjectivism, which holds that knowledge and truth are not independent of human existence.

(Darvill, 2008)

An example of an objective statement is: 'The netsuke in the British Museum is 4.7 cm long.' And a subjective statement might run: 'The netsuke in the British Museum is beautiful.' The former is an independently verifiable observation; the latter is an emotional response to the object. It's not a question of rightness or wrongness: it is a question of which is the appropriate form of description for the current purpose. So if you are describing an object in your academic study, or so that someone else can have as clear as possible an idea of the appearance of an object, then an objective description of an object is appropriate. If on the other hand you are discussing an object in an informal way, or describing the effect an object has had on you, then a subjective description might be appropriate: 'It was impressive and awe-inspiring.'

Activity

Here are seven statements about the netsuke in the British Museum. Sort them into objective and subjective groups.

1 The netsuke is undamaged.

2 The netsuke is made of ivory.

3 The netsuke is in the shape of an elephant.

4 The netsuke is an exquisite piece of workmanship.

5 The netsuke is made from a single piece of ivory.

6 The netsuke is valuable.

7 The netsuke is not a forgery.

You should allow about 10 minutes for this activity.

Discussion

Some of these statements are easier to categorise than others. Where the boundary between subjectivity and objectivity lies is often debatable. Here are my comments on each statement:

1   The netsuke is undamaged.

    This is an objective judgement: there are no obvious signs of wear or breakages, and the netsuke appears to be complete. An expert object conservator might identify small imperfections, but whether these matter depends on the reason for identifying them. Once we begin thinking about the extent of the damage, we are becoming more subjective in our thinking.

2   The netsuke is made of ivory.

    This is also objective: apparently the netsuke is all made of the same material and it looks like ivory. Scientific tests could determine the type of ivory – for example, is it elephant ivory, or hippopotamus ivory?

3   The netsuke is in the shape of an elephant.

    Well, this sounds objective. But actually we need to be careful, because although the netsuke is recognisable as an elephant, it is not a perfect miniature copy of one. The person who created it was working within an artistic tradition that has stylistic conventions (for example, the heads of the elephant and the men are more rounded than is natural). Identifying the netsuke as being 'in the shape of an elephant' is, strictly, a subjective judgement because the process of identification is an act of interpretation.

4   The netsuke is an exquisite piece of workmanship.

    This is a subjective judgement: we can argue about what makes something 'exquisite' for as long as we like.

5   The netsuke is made from a single piece of ivory.

    This is objective so long as we agree that the netsuke is made of ivory, and careful examination should enable us to observe whether it was made from a single piece.

6   The netsuke is valuable.

    This is largely a subjective statement. In monetary terms the ivory has an intrinsic value. It probably derives more value from its status as a rare and antique artefact: this is its aesthetic value.

7   The netsuke is not a forgery.

    This, too, is a subjective statement, since we are dependent on the opinions of specialists to judge the netsuke's authenticity. However, the statement might be objective if there were some incontrovertible proof that it is not a forgery.

These statements are a mixed bag, with very few that can be confidently classed as objective once they are examined in detail. Some scholars are doubtful of the usefulness of distinguishing between subjective and objective, arguing that even apparently objective observations are dependent on the judgement of the observer who makes them, or on the accuracy of their observations, and that objective facts which are independent of someone observing them cannot exist.

Defining subjectivity and objectivity is ultimately a philosophical problem. But if we reformulate the difference as the difference between opinion and fact, or between assertion and argument supported by evidence, its importance to studying material culture becomes clear. If we are reading about an object, we can analyse what we read by asking, 'Is it assertion or is it fact?' A statement such as 'The netsuke is valuable' is an assertion; it is someone else's opinion. In contrast, a statement such as 'DNA analysis indicates the netsuke is made of elephant ivory' is a statement supported by evidence. We might then wish to follow up the statement by checking evidence, perhaps tracing it to its source by locating a scientific report produced by a recognised DNA laboratory. When we come to write about the netsuke we can be careful to avoid unsupported assertions; so, rather than writing subjectively, 'The netsuke is valuable', we can be more objective and precise by writing, 'The netsuke has a high monetary value: in 2006 a netsuke by the same artist sold for £1440 at a Sotheby's auction in London.' In this way we are writing a statement and then providing both evidence to support that statement and also the source of the information.

Descriptions or analyses can be categorised as either objective or subjective, but there are other ways to categorise them. Another interesting difference is that between an **etic** and an **emic** description (see box).

Etic and emic

An *etic* description is one made from outside a culture and an *emic* description is one made from inside a culture. So if you or a museum curator describes the netsuke, then that is an etic description. If a nineteenth-century Japanese craftsman were to have described the same object, then that would be an emic description.

In practical terms it is difficult to find emic descriptions for historical or archaeological objects, because either they have not been described or such descriptions have not survived. It is more feasible to find emic descriptions for ethnographic objects (objects from living societies) or contemporary items of material culture.

In summary, the important points to remember are that in addition to the form, function and uses of an object, an object also has a context, whether original (when the object was made) or contemporary (where the object is now), and can embody ideas and concepts. How all of these qualities influence people, or how people exploit them, constitutes the 'social life' of an object. Context will be explored more fully in the next chapter.

2.3 Classifying Greek vases

In this section we shall focus on the (modern) classification of ancient Greek vases. The information is presented in the form of a life cycle, structured by production, consumption and afterlife. You are familiar with this methodology both from your work in Chapter 1 and from earlier in this chapter, where the model was explored in relation to the biography of a Japanese elephant netsuke. One additional aim of this section, then, is to develop your existing understanding of the life-cycle concept, providing you with an ancient example to set alongside the objects you have considered so far. Remember that the life cycle (in contrast to the individual object biography) applies to a whole category of objects, and therefore entails some degree of generalisation.

Production

Vases were made in many places in ancient Greece, notably in Attica, the region around Athens. Many of the Attic vases surviving today were made in the *Kerameikos* (the source of our modern word 'ceramic'): the potters' quarter of Athens, located to the northwest of the city's Acropolis. We have very little written evidence relating to Greek vases and workshops, so much of our information about their production comes from close analysis of the pots themselves, from excavations of ancient kilns, or from images which show potters and painters in action. Figure 2.4, for instance, shows a craftsman seated on a stool, painting a large pot that rests on his knee; we can imagine him dipping his brush into the dish on the low table by his side. Note that the objects hanging above him indicate that we are in the interior space of a workshop. The pot he is painting is known as a *krater* (a bowl for mixing wine); indeed, this scene is itself painted on to a 'real' *krater*.

The production of an Athenian vase began with the digging of clay from a clay bed and its transportation to a workshop where it was prepared for working into a pot. It was then turned on a wheel or a turntable, or worked completely by hand on a fixed base, gradually taking on the form of a vase. A great variety of vase shapes were produced in Attic workshops, and you can see the most common types in the diagram at Figure 2.5. Some shapes could be made out of a single piece of clay, but most would be made in sections before being stuck together. In modern labelling, the different elements of Greek

Figure 2.4 Attic red-figure *krater* by the Komaris Painter, detail showing a potter painting a *krater*, *c*.430–425 BCE. Ashmolean Museum, Oxford. Photo: Ashmolean Museum, University of Oxford/The Bridgeman Art Library

vases correspond to parts of the human body – a vase can have shoulders, a belly and ears (handles), as well as a lip, mouth and neck.

After shaping, the vessel was decorated. Often the painter of the vase was a different person from the potter, although sometimes the same

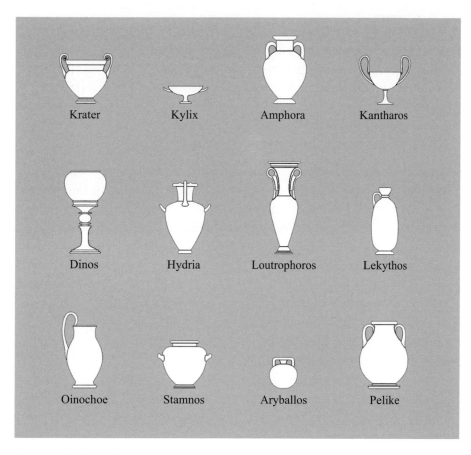

Figure 2.5 This diagram shows some of the most common Greek vase shapes

person both shaped and decorated the piece. The vase was decorated using a fine clay **slip** – that is, a liquid mixture of clay and water which would eventually turn black during the firing process. This slip was made from the same clay as the body of the vase, but was more finely filtered. At the moment the decoration was applied, then, the slip and vase would have been the same natural clay colour. This makes the painter's achievement all the more impressive, since he could not easily have seen what he was drawing. It is possible that he first outlined the scene in charcoal, which would then have burned away during the firing process. Firing the pot and reducing the oxygen in the kiln, during a three-stage process, had the effect of 'fixing' the coloured areas of the vase. This is how Attic vases achieved their distinctive red and black colours.

The most famous and widespread techniques of vase decoration were called 'black-figure' and 'red-figure'. **Black-figure painting** was developed in Corinth in the seventh century BCE, while **red-figure painting** was probably invented in Athens around 530 BCE. In black-figure scenes, as you might expect, the people and other elements are represented in black, while the background of the scene is red. Red-figure reverses this colour scheme, so that the people appear in red and the background in black. You can see examples of both techniques in the illustrations in this section (for example, Figures 2.6 and 2.7).

After the vases were removed from the kiln, extra paint was sometimes added. (If you look ahead at the *krater* in Figure 2.10, for instance, you can see rich red blood pouring from the dead man's body.) White paint was also used for contrast and gender differentiation; in particular, women's bodies were frequently painted white to reflect classical Greek ideals of female beauty.

Consumption

Attic pots were used as all kinds of containers, from jewellery boxes and perfume bottles to industrial-scale storage jars used to transport substances such as wine, water, honey, grain and olive oil. Again, the images on vases can help us to appreciate the range of ways in which the pots were used. The black-figure side of the bilingual amphora (a basic storage vessel for liquids) pictured in Figure 2.6 shows the demi-god Herakles holding a *kantharos* (a drinking vessel with high handles), which has been filled from the *dinos* (a bowl for mixing wine which has its own separate stand) to the right of the scene. We also have many vases depicting scenes of a 'symposium', or drinking party for elite male citizens, during which a great variety of different vessels were used. Figure 2.8, for example, shows drinkers playing a typical game called *kottabos*, which involved flicking wine at a target: here each of the reclining men twirls a *kylix* (a shallow drinking cup), while a *krater* is suspended between them.

Other pots had special ritual uses: the *loutrophoros*, for instance, was a tall vessel with an elongated neck and two handles that was used to hold the water for marriage and funerary rituals. The similarly shaped *lekythos* was also used in funerary rituals, but this time to carry the oil that was offered at the grave. Sometimes these ritual vessels are found inside the graves themselves, while larger marble versions of both shapes were used as grave-markers.

Another point regarding use relates to the idea of affordability; while Greek vases fetch huge sums on the modern antiques market, in ancient

Figure 2.6 Black-figure side of a bilingual amphora by the Andokides Painter, showing the demi-god Herakles feasting, *c*.520 BCE. Staatliche Antikensammlugen und Glyptothek, Munich. Photo: Christa Koppermann

object represented – in this case, a continuation of an ancient tradition, a connection with the classical past – was important in that object's value and can continue to influence later generations.

Afterlife

This brings us neatly on to the post-antique afterlife of Attic vases. After excavation from Etruscan tombs, most pots eventually found their way into museums (although many have also been bought and sold on the illegal antiquities market). In a museum, their display on pedestals or in cases behind glass transforms them into untouchable treasures. The written label displayed next to each vase traditionally states the date and provenance of the piece, describes its shape and the subject painted, and sometimes gives the artist's name, but rarely is any mention made of its original function, or of material properties such as its weight or the volume of liquid that it could hold. Moreover, the simple statement of provenance ('from Vulci', for example) often conceals a long and sometimes troubled post-excavation history. The vases shown in Figure 2.9, for instance, are now in the British Museum, but were bought in Italy in the eighteenth century by Sir William Hamilton (1730–1803), who was then the British ambassador to Naples. The more fragmentary vases to the right of the photograph were among those loaded on to the British naval ship HMS *Colossus*, which subsequently sank on its way back to Britain. These vases were

Figure 2.9 Vases from the second collection of Sir William Hamilton, photograph. British Museum, London. Photo: The Trustees of the British Museum

recovered only in the 1970s, after more than 200 years on the seabed. Here they are shown reunited with other vases from Hamilton's collection which had arrived in London two centuries earlier, after a rather less eventful journey.

Meanwhile, the *krater* shown in Figure 2.10 was the first Greek vase to be sold for a million dollars. In 1972 it was bought from a private dealer by the then director of the New York Metropolitan Museum of Art, Thomas Hoving (1931–2009), but was repatriated to Italy in 2006 amid huge controversy. Hoving wrote a gripping account of the afterlife of the 'New York hot pot' (as the vase became known in the press). If you want some lighter reading about the afterlives of vases, then you

Figure 2.10 The Euphronios vase, a red-figure *krater* showing the body of Sarpedon, son of the chief Greek god Zeus and a hero of the Trojan war, being carried by the personifications of Sleep and Death, *c.*515 BCE. Museo di Villa Giulia, Rome. Photo: Scala, Florence. Reproduced courtesy of the Ministero Beni e Att. Culturali

might try this mixture of public scandal and detective story, which – apart from anything else – shows the level of passion and intrigue that Greek pots can inspire. It certainly shows the importance of relative values and affordability; although not of high value in its original context, the subsequent afterlife of the vase adds a huge amount to its value, in monetary terms.

Greek vases and photographs of Greek vases are also a valuable source of evidence for students and scholars. The pots themselves can be subject to chemical and physical analysis, which can tell us about the provenance and mineral composition of the clay from which they were made, as well as techniques of manufacture. The fact that decorated Attic pots can normally be dated to within a quarter of a century is immensely useful to archaeologists – even a tiny fragment of pottery can help to establish the date of the building or site where it was found. The visual imagery on the pots, studied either first-hand or by using photographs, can be used to reconstruct largely lost forms of Greek art such as wall- and panel-painting. Used carefully, such imagery can also give us some fascinating insights into ancient life and thought. The images in this section alone shed light on Greek ideas about divinity, heroism and gender, and represent practices as diverse as bronze-working and drunken feasting. In recent decades Greek vases have also been mined for information about the lives of women, who are marginalised in Greek and Latin texts but who appear in their thousands in the red and black scenes of Attic pottery.

Each generation of students and scholars finds something new in this rich body of material, and the same is true of the many writers and artists who have made new creations based on ancient Greek vases. Figure 2.11 depicts one of the Wedgwood company's neoclassical vases, which gives a distinctive nineteenth-century twist to the classical source material.

Activity

You should allow about 30 minutes for this activity.

Read back over the life cycle described here, and then examine the images of Greek vases illustrated throughout this section, together with their captions. As you do so, think about how Attic vases might be classified by scholars. You should aim to come up with at least two different ways of grouping the material (a hint: alphabetical and autobiographical criteria are unlikely to work here).

Figure 2.11 Vase with cover, black basalt, with painting of Dionysus (the god of wine and drunken revelry) and maenad (one of his female followers), by Josiah Wedgwood and Sons Ltd, nineteenth century. Victoria and Albert Museum, London, #2412&A–1901. Photo: © Victoria and Albert Museum, London

Discussion

Here are some of the ways in which Attic vases might be classified. The list is not exhaustive and you may well have thought of different criteria.

Vase shape

Shape is commonly used by scholars as a way of dividing Attic vases into groups. Most introductory textbooks on classical art contain a diagram similar to the one reproduced in Figure 2.5, which illustrates twelve possible categories of vase shape for the diligent student to commit to memory. Once they have done so, any new vase encountered in an excavation, museum or library can be identified instantly, and labelled as a *kylix*, or a *krater*, and so on. The number of categories within the classification can vary: a simple classification might have only two categories, reflecting a broad division between 'open' shapes (such as *kraters* and *stamnoi*) and 'closed' shapes (such as *amphorae* and *oinochoi*); at the other end of the spectrum we could choose to subdivide each shape into all its possible varieties, and thereby produce a classification with dozens of categories of vase shape.

Technique of decoration

This is another very common and intuitive type of classification. Books on Greek vases are often divided into chapters on red-figure painting, black-figure painting and other, less common techniques such as **white-ground painting**. You probably now feel confident in your ability to recognise a vase as either black-figure or red-figure – every time you do so, you are performing an act of mental classification.

Date

Classifying vases according to the period in which they were made is another possibility. Again, anyone choosing to impose this classification on the material would need to decide the size and number of categories to use: they could divide the vases into those made in the sixth century BCE, the fifth century, fourth century, and so on; or they could subdivide each century into, for instance, 25-year periods. Their choice might depend on the number of vases available to classify, and the precision with which they are to be dated. Note that studying the style of the painting can help with chronology. For instance, as mentioned earlier, red-figure painting was probably developed around 530 BCE, so we think we know that any red-figure vase must have been made after this date.

Findspot

Attic vases by definition were made in Attica, so the place of manufacture is not a particularly useful classification here (of course, if the activity had asked you to classify vases from all over Greece, then place of production would have been a useful criterion of classification). However, Attic vases can be classified according to the place where they were found (their 'findspot'), providing that this information is available – so, for example, vases found in the Etruscan city of Vulci can be grouped in a different category from those found at the nearby site of Tarquinia. Note that this form of classification privileges the reception or afterlife stage of a vessel's life cycle.

Museum collection

The current location of vases is another straightforward way in which they can be pigeonholed. So, again, we might imagine a book about vases being divided into chapters on 'Vases in the Fitzwilliam Museum in Cambridge', 'Vases in the Metropolitan Museum of Art in New York', and so forth.

Artist

Classification by artist was relatively common in the early part of the twentieth century. The artist or potter would sometimes sign their work, making it fairly straightforward to identify them. However, many vases are not signed. In these cases, the artist is sometimes identified through close examination of details of style, and nicknames (such as the Perseus Painter) are given to an anonymous artist identifiable through particular stylistic details. This type of classification certainly had an effect on the value of specific pieces, although these days it is considered less reliable. However, you may still find this approach in some earlier writings on the subject. One particular exponent of this approach was Sir John Davidson Beazley (1885–1970).

Subject

Classification by the type of scene represented on the vase is increasingly popular in the world of scholarship. Vases might be divided into representations of, say, the symposium, or athletes, or musicians. This mode of classification allows us to compare representations of similar events or activities, and observe how these representations developed over time.

Conclusion

This chapter opened with a rich field of human activity: making music. It quickly became apparent how challenging it is to begin to impose classification on the objects and qualities associated with music. You were introduced to some possible solutions, but, as with the example of the record collection in the film *High Fidelity*, any solution depends on your definition of the problem. The case study of the netsuke allowed you to work carefully through the ways in which descriptions can be created and used within systems of classification. You have already learned that the key to description is observing, interpreting and then communicating your observations. You have also worked with a museum's collections database and can apply your experience the next time you use a museum website that offers public access to its collections database. You completed this chapter by investigating the life cycle and the challenges of classifying Greek vases.

You now know quite a lot about the ways that music can be classified, how classification makes sense of unfamiliar objects, and about the production, consumption and afterlife of Attic vases. We hope this knowledge will enrich your future encounters with these types of object, and encourage you to think about all the other people who have encountered them before you – from the historical creator, to the collector, curator and scholar in modern times.

More generally, your work in this chapter has emphasised that there is no 'natural' way of classifying a collection of objects, and that analysis of any classification we choose can often reveal a particular system of values or beliefs. This idea is one that you should try to apply to other classifications of material culture, as and when you meet them. Next time you open a book about art or archaeology, or next time you go into a museum or to an online database, you should pause to identify and then interrogate how the collection has been organised (into, for example, chapters, galleries or search terms). Try asking yourself the following three questions:

- Which elements of the objects, and which parts of their life histories, does this classification privilege?

- What are the academic trends and the broader cultural beliefs that underpin this classification?

- And what alternative ways might there be of ordering the material?

We hope your answers to these questions will reveal some interesting things about 'things', and about the people who collect, study and (re) present them.

References

Best, A. (2005) '"Our respective empires should stand together": the royal dimension in Anglo-Japanese relations, 1919–1941', *Diplomacy & Statecraft*, vol. 16, no. 2, pp. 259–79.

British Museum (2009) *Report and Accounts for the Year Ended 31 March 2009* [Online], London, The Stationery Office. Available at http://www.britishmuseum.org/pdf/TAR08_09.pdf (Accessed 10 March 2014).

Daily Telegraph (2005) 'Royal heirlooms for sale to pay death duties', 14 November [Online]. Available at http://www.telegraph.co.uk/news/uknews/1502913/Royal-heirlooms-for-sale-to-pay-death-duties.html (Accessed 10 March 2014).

Darvill, T. (2008) 'Objectivity', in *The Concise Oxford Dictionary of Archaeology* [Online], Oxford, Oxford University Press. Available at http://www.oxfordreference.com/views/ENTRY.html?subview=Main&entry=t102.e2812 (Accessed 10 March 2014).

High Fidelity (2000) Directed by Stephen Frears [Film]. Burbank, CA, Touchstone Pictures.

Saxe, J.G. (1873) *The Poems of John Godfrey Saxe*, Boston, MA, James R. Osgood and Co.

Further reading

If you would like to read more about netsuke and see some fabulous examples, Barbra Teri Okada (1980) provides a survey of the art form. For a detailed and authoritative introduction to Greek vases, John Boardman (2008) is the place to start, although the topic is so vast one book is not enough. Thomas Hoving (2001) provides an account of the afterlife of the 'New York hot pot'.

Boardman, J. (2008) *The Greek Vase: Art of the Storyteller*, London, Thames & Hudson.

Hoving, T. (2001) 'Super art gems of New York City: the grand and glorious "hot pot" – will Italy snag it?', *Artnet*, June–July [Online]. Available at www.artnet.com/Magazine/features/hoving/hoving6-29-01.asp (Accessed 10 March 2014).

Okada, B.T. (1980) 'Netsuke: the small sculptures of Japan', *The Metropolitan Museum of Art Bulletin*, New Series, vol. 38, no. 2, pp. 2–48 [Online]. Available at http://www.jstor.org/stable/3258709 (Accessed 19 February 2014).

Chapter 3
Contexts of material culture

Phil Perkins

Contents

Aims

This chapter will:

- introduce you to the concept of context as used in Archaeology and Anthropology
- develop your skills of observation and description
- develop your understanding of ethnographic context
- develop your understanding of archaeological context
- introduce you to the study of groups of objects.

Materials you will need

In this chapter, you will need the following reading, which can be found through the module website:

- Vincentelli, M. (1989) 'Reflections on a Kabyle pot: Algerian women and the decorative tradition', *Journal of Design History*, vol. 2, nos 2/3, pp. 123–38.

You will also be directed to the website for an online activity.

Introduction

In the last chapter you considered ways of describing individual objects, identifying their functions and classifying them. Your work highlighted the fact that studying an object in isolation produces a limited interpretation. However, studying an object alongside related objects, ideas and circumstances can produce a subtler and broader interpretation.

In this chapter, we shall be looking at how 'context' is understood and used within Material Culture Studies, and specifically within Archaeology and Anthropology. The humanities use the idea of 'context' widely, typically to discuss the circumstances surrounding an object or a text, such as Elizabethan attitudes to learning and religion in a study of the play *Doctor Faustus* (you will have already encountered these ideas if you have studied AA100 *The arts past and present*). This chapter uses 'context' as the term for all the surrounding objects, ideas and physical circumstances associated with an object. In the case of material culture, context is primarily about relationships between objects and their environment, past and present.

Chapter 1 used the example of the Pitt Rivers Museum in Oxford to consider how the way that the objects were displayed there related to Pitt Rivers' theories about cultural evolution. The objects came from different cultures and different historical periods but were displayed together on the basis of their physical similarities. Each object came from an original cultural context (the society that created it) and gained a new context in relation to its place in the museum display. An understanding of why the objects were grouped together in this nineteenth-century museum can be reached by reading Pitt Rivers' texts about his theories. However, these texts have little to say about the objects in their original contexts. The ways we can learn about original contexts differ – sometimes we have direct first-hand information; at other times we have to depend on what we can learn from the objects themselves. This chapter will explore these ways of knowing about and understanding objects in society.

In this chapter you will be investigating two aspects of context: ethnographic context and archaeological context. Anthropologists use ethnographic methods with living societies. Investigating ethnographic context, as in your work on Kula valuables in Chapter 1, entails finding the people who made an object, visiting them, and observing and asking them about the object and the role it performs in their society and culture. Investigating archaeological context entails studying objects that were found alongside the object of interest and also establishing and examining the circumstances and conditions in which the object was found, for example considering *where* it was found. There are other aspects to context, for instance the historical context (the historical circumstances related to an object), or the cultural context or social context – which you will consider in more detail in Chapter 4 of this book, and in later books. Context is not a fixed and permanent set of circumstances; it can change as objects move through time and space, as, for example, Greek vases have moved from Athens in the fifth century BCE to their present-day context in twenty-first century London. A context can also become more detailed and specific the more it is investigated and researched and can help to provide a richer interpretation of an object.

In the first part of this chapter you will be using and developing your skills of observation and description to infer the functions and interpretation of some objects (pottery from Kabyle villages in Algeria, north Africa) that are likely to be unfamiliar to you. This will help you to apply these skills when you meet other new material objects. At the same time you will be looking beyond the individual objects you encounter to focus on the various contexts through which they have passed.

The second part of the chapter focuses on studying the Roman city of Pompeii, Italy, buried by ashes from the volcano Mount Vesuvius in 79 CE. In the case of Pompeii it is possible to study and interpret a whole group of objects found together. Finally, by working through the online activity you will be able to examine objects in their ancient context and have more opportunities to interpret what has been found.

3.1 The ethnographic approach

To start your work on context, you will begin by studying an object that will probably be unfamiliar to you. You will therefore be depending on your skills of observation and description to work towards an interpretation of the object. Studying the object in isolation will take you only so far; to achieve a greater understanding of the object it will be necessary to find out about its context. To explore its context you will be taking an ethnographic approach, because similar objects are still being made and used in the world today.

Activity

Look at Figure 3.1. Observe it closely and write a description based on your close observation. Try to use about 500 words, so you can go into some detail. In your description try to include the following: the shape and size of the object, the different parts that make it up, the material it is made of, how it was made, its colour, its decoration (how this appears, where it is, how it was done) and any areas where it has been damaged. Finally, try to identify the object by providing a name for it that you think is suitable and try to suggest its function You could use the following headings to help: 'Shape', 'Material', 'Decoration' and 'Interpretation'.

You should allow about 30 minutes for this activity.

Discussion

Here are some comments on how I set about writing my description. Some parts of the list of things to observe and describe are easier to pick out than others. I'll discuss each part of the description before providing my own version at the end of this discussion.

Shape

The shape is difficult to describe, and it is not always easy to be precise when working from a photograph. Rather than try to describe every aspect of the shape, I would probably accept the (obvious enough) observation that the object is some sort of vase or pot. Of course, this observation is entirely based on my prior knowledge of vases: it looks a bit like other vases I have seen. Like these other vases, this one has a circular footprint and it keeps this circular shape as its width varies from the bottom to the top. By recognising that the object is similar to something else, the description will become easier to understand (and write), because certain aspects of its shape will conform to our shared expectations about what a vase is usually like. It may also help to use analogies, for example noting that the vase is 'almond-shaped' or 'eye-shaped' (it could also be described as 'acorn-shaped' or 'egg-shaped').

117

Figure 3.1 Ceramic object, height 50cm, width 22.5cm. Victoria and Albert Museum 31:12-1868. Photo © Victoria and Albert Museum, London

The size is given in the figure caption. If the object were in front of you it would be possible to measure it directly; in the caption you have dimensions for the height and width, but other measurements could also be given (for example the diameter of the mouth of the vase, the diameter of the foot and other details of the decoration could also be measured to help create a precise description).

The vase could be described by dividing it into parts. It has a foot or base, then there is the main body, and above that a neck and a mouth. (You saw in Chapter 2 that terms derived from the human body can be useful in describing an inanimate object.) The vase also has two handles on opposite sides of the body. The shape of the handles is difficult to describe, but the one on the left has what looks like an in-turned horn shape. The top of the other one is broken.

Material

The caption states that the vase is ceramic, but that is only really observable when we are looking at the 'real thing'. From the photograph it is difficult to say how the pot was made: ceramics are usually either **handmade**, **wheel-turned** or made in a mould. This one looks slightly irregular in shape so it may well be handmade, but it is impossible to tell without inspecting the object. The handles were probably handmade and then attached to the body of the pot.

Decoration

The decoration is complex, so perhaps it is best to describe it in general terms and then focus on details. Making a differentiation between the decoration and the shape or material of an object is not always easy. Here, the horn-shaped handles could be considered as decoration and the appearance of the clay material could easily be considered as decorative. The word 'decoration' usually means something that has no function other than to look interesting or to embellish an object. Yet 'decoration' could also convey meanings and be significant in some way as well.

Interpretation

Here, 'interpretation' means using your observations to arrive at a more general understanding of the object – perhaps identifying its function and so giving it a name, or using your prior knowledge to interpret your observations and identify the object.

You can read my final description in the accompanying box. Compare it with yours and see if the two generally match. At what points do they differ? Is there more or less detail in your description? I suspect that my description may be more detailed than yours because it attempts to describe even the smallest parts of the decoration.

Description of the object in Figure 3.1

Shape

This is a ceramic vessel 50cm tall, standing on a flared circular foot. Above the foot the vase becomes narrower before widening to form an egg-shaped body and then narrowing again to form a neck, above which the vase widens once more to form a flaring mouth. On either side of the vase a curved handle is attached at the widest point on the body. The upper part of each handle is attached to the shoulder of the vase by a strut; above this the handle continues upwards, curving in towards the neck to form a cow's-horn-like shape. This part of the handle is broken off on the right handle. The space between the body and the handles forms an inverted teardrop shape.

The vase has a circular footprint and a slightly uneven profile, so the body may have been made by hand or possibly on a potter's wheel, with the handles attached later.

Material

The vase is made from buff-coloured clay that has been smoothed to produce a shiny surface and then painted with red and black paint. It is not possible to describe the material in great detail working from the photograph alone.

Decoration

The vase is decorated with horizontal bands of dark red and beige, slightly glossy paint, separated by black outlines. The beige areas are further decorated by fine black lines, perhaps painted with a fine brush, and black dots – possibly fingerprints.

Starting from the bottom, the base is dark red with a broad beige band above which has a thick black outline. Just inside the outlines are thinner horizontal black lines and between these is a triple zigzag line. All the painted lines, here and elsewhere, are somewhat uneven: they are neither straight nor evenly spaced. Above this is a dark red band occupying the narrowest part of the base of the vase. Above this on the lower part of the body is a broad beige band with thick black outlines and again thin black lines just inside the outlines. Just above and below the thin lines is an uneven row of black dots, in some cases overlapping the thin line.

In the centre of the body, between the two handles, is an uneven, roughly rectangular panel whose sides follow the curves of the body of the vessel. The panel is beige and the surrounding body is dark red; they are separated by a thick black line with a thinner black line on the inner edge of the panel. This panel is divided into nine unequal rectangular parts forming a cross-like overall design. The upper row of three rectangles consists of a pair of almost square shapes separated by two thin vertical black lines from a tall rectangle in the centre. This central rectangle is decorated with nine horizontal uneven zigzag lines. The square shapes to either side are similar to one another. In each square a triple thin black line marks a 'V' shape, leaving a beige triangle in each of the lower corners of the square. Above the 'V' are two beige diamond shapes outlined with a thin black line; the remainder of the space above the 'V' is filled with diagonal cross-hatched lines. The middle row of three rectangles consists of a pair of long rectangles separated by two thin vertical black lines from a small square in the centre that is decorated to form a black and beige chequerboard pattern. The rectangles on either side are similar to the squares above, decorated with a 'V' shape, but the entire area above the 'V' is filled with diagonal cross-hatched lines. The lower row of three rectangles is very similar to the upper row, except that the area above the 'V' shapes in each of the squares is filled with four diamond shapes arranged in a row of three in the upper part with one below fitting into the point of the 'V'; these diamonds are filled with diagonal cross-hatched lines.

Above the central panel and just above the handles is a beige band with black painting very similar to that around the foot. The lower part of the handles is beige, separated from the dark red background by the usual thick and thin black outline, and the handles are each decorated with five black spots. The neck and mouth are plain dark red in colour.

Interpretation

The two-handled vessel or vase, perhaps a jar, is presumably intended to contain a liquid. The size of the vase suggests that it may have been designed to store a liquid, but the handles and mouth suggest it would also have been used for pouring the liquid.

This is a long description for a single vase – it is nearer 775 words than the 500 that you were allocated. The decoration in particular was very difficult to describe accurately. I think it would still be quite hard for someone who has not seen the vase to visualise it accurately from this description alone. Note that descriptions can also draw the reader's attention to particular features of an object: perhaps there is some aspect of the vase that you hadn't observed before reading my description. On the other hand, you may have spent more time describing a detail that I have skimmed over.

Comparison in the museum context

So far we have been studying this vase in isolation: it has been entirely decontextualised and has no associated biography. All that we have observed, described and interpreted has been entirely confined to information contained in the object itself. This may help us understand some of its biography: how it was made and decorated, for example. We might make a reasonable guess at its current location in a museum, but to try to understand more about the vase we need to discover and explore more of its context.

Activity

Compare the object in Figure 3.2 with the one in Figure 3.1 that you have just described. Note down some similarities and some differences between the two ceramic vessels.

Discussion

The vessels are very different shapes, which might perhaps be due to their having different functions. Nonetheless, there is some vague resemblance between the shape of the foot of both vessels. The decoration of the two objects is also similar, with a dark red background and beige panels outlined in black and filled with fine black lines forming 'V', triangle and diamond shapes. Although it is not possible to argue that the two vessels are 'the same', the level of similarity suggests that they may have been made in the same place, at around the same time, and that they were probably made in a similar way and possibly by the same group of people – or even by the same person.

The two vessels share a contemporary context: at the present stage of their biographies they share a shelf in a display case in Room 145 in the

Figure 3.2 Kabyle *mesbah* (oil lamp), Algeria, before 1868, earthenware, decorated with kaolin, coloured oxides and slips, and covered with resin. Victoria and Albert Museum 31:48-1868. Photo © Victoria and Albert Museum, London

Victoria and Albert Museum in London, alongside a similar third vessel. These objects have been placed together because of their similarities. As you might imagine, the museum has gathered information about them, including details of when they entered the museum and where they came from.

This museum documentation identifies the vase in Figure 3.1 as a jar and the one in Figure 3.2 as an oil lamp. These are etic descriptions, because they are made by people external to the society that made and first used the objects. However, the museum labels also provide other names for them: *tekelilt* and *mesbah*, respectively. These are emic descriptions, the names given to these vase shapes by the Kabyle people (a Berber ethnic group who live in the mountainous area of Grande Kabylie in Algeria, north Africa, to the southeast of Algiers), using their own language. (To remind yourself of etic and emic descriptions, refer back to Chapter 2, Section 2.2.)

Searching the museum's database reveals that it has 22 similar vases. These appear to have been acquired by the museum at the same time, and all have similar details written about them. The descriptions provide a few general details about the people who made the vessels, but there is not much in-depth information.

Exploring the Kabyle context

To discover more about the original context of vases like these at an earlier stage of their biographies it would be necessary to look elsewhere to find a book, academic article or internet resource written about the Kabyle people or Kabyle ceramics. In 1982 Moira Vincentelli (Emeritus Professor in Art History and Curator of Ceramics at Aberystwyth University) visited Algeria to undertake some ethnographic research and to meet the women who still make similar pottery. She wrote up her research and it was published in an academic journal in 1989 (Vincentelli, 1989). Shortly you will be reading part of this article, but before you do a few comments on reading an academic article will be helpful (see box).

Scan-reading academic texts

Academic articles often go into great detail about a specific topic, but it is often possible to quickly gather an impression of what the article is about without having to read it all. Once you have a general impression you can then decide whether to spend more time reading all, or just some of the article. Here are some suggestions of what to look for:

- Title: a good title should tell you what the article is about and should enable you to assess its relevance to your study.

- Abstracts: if you are lucky, an article will be preceded by an abstract. This consists of a few sentences which very briefly summarise the article and point out the major conclusions.

- Introduction: a good article will have an introduction that lets you know what the article is about and how it is structured.

- Conclusions: the last part of an article will often summarise the whole article and make clear the overall conclusions or the significance of what has been discussed. Reading the conclusions first can save time.

- Sections/subheadings: articles will often be divided into sections with subheadings. Quickly looking through and reading these subheadings should give you an impression of how the article is structured and the overall shape of its argument.

- Beginnings and endings: quickly reading the beginning and ending of a section should give you an idea of what the section contains; there may even be a brief summary or conclusion at the end of each section.

- Evidence/data: a central section, perhaps following the introduction, will discuss the evidence or sources on which the arguments of the article are based. This section will be useful to read if you need to analyse the argument in detail.

Scan-reading will give you an impression of the issues and topics discussed in the article. However, it is not the same as actually reading the whole article and will give you just that: an impression. It may not accurately reflect the full content and arguments of the article.

Vincentelli's article starts by generally introducing the Kabyle people and their traditional methods of making pottery. It then goes on to provide a discussion of the function and meaning of the vases. You will see that this quite closely matches the processes of description, identifying function and interpretation that you explored in Chapter 2. You will be reading this article in sections so that you can focus on individual aspects of the ethnographic context of the Kabyle ceramics. In the various sections you will study the relationships between people and the things they make and use, the ways the things are designed and decorated, and any meanings or significance which they contain or communicate. In essence you will be studying the relationships between things, people and their society – a central theme of this module. All these relationships constitute parts of the context of the objects.

Activity

You should allow about 20 minutes for this activity.

You will find a link to Moira Vincentelli's article, 'Reflections on a Kabyle pot: Algerian women and the decorative tradition', on the module website. The article was originally published in the *Journal of Design History* (1989), vol. 2, nos 2/3, pp. 123–38. If you have not already done so, find this article now.

Read the first two sections of the article, stopping when you reach the beginning of the section headed 'Kabyle pottery-making and decorative traditions' on p. 124. You may find that taking notes which summarise the content of the article will help you to clearly see the different aspects of context that are discussed. What aspects of the context of the Kabyle ceramics are discussed in these first two sections?

Discussion

After providing a brief outline of the article Vincentelli introduces the Kabylie and Kabyle society, identifying one aspect of the context of the ceramics as the domestic environment in the villages of Kabylie in Algeria. This constitutes part of the broader social, geographical and political context of the pottery and the people who made it. Vincentelli then introduces the academic context of the study of Kabyle ceramics, mentioning some previous academic studies of these ceramics that represent the state of knowledge about the subject at that time. The next section, 'African ceramics and western taste' (p. 124), goes on to situate the ceramics within the more general cultural context of western art. To some extent this section is justifying the study of objects that are not traditionally considered as art, and setting these objects apart from art objects. The question of what is and isn't art is an interesting and complex one, but it need not slow us down here, because our focus is on material culture more generally – a category which includes both 'art' and 'craft' regardless of how we define these terms.

Activity

Now read the next section, 'Kabyle pottery-making and decorative traditions' (p. 124), stopping when you reach the beginning of the section headed 'Meaning and function of Kabyle ceramics' on p. 126. Continue taking notes which summarise the content of the article. What aspects of the context of the Kabyle ceramics are discussed in this section?

You should allow about 20 minutes for this activity.

Discussion

Here there is more discussion about the social context, in terms of a community of relatively isolated villages and more specifically as part of the world of female activities in a village community. Potting and some other crafts are identified as gendered activities undertaken by women, whereas other activities are undertaken by men. The local economic context of craft production is also briefly introduced, along with the technological context describing the resources, technology and know-how required to make the pottery. The last part of this section focuses on the visual aspects of the cultural context, describing how the making and decorating of the pottery is related to other crafts such as basketry, house-painting and tattooing, which use the same decorative motifs.

In the first three sections of the article Vincentelli discusses various aspects of the context of the Kabyle pots and their manufacture and decoration. In the next section she explores the functions of the pots, the meaning that their decoration might contain and how this might be interpreted: she is trying to interpret the material culture.

Activity

Read the next, longer, section of Vincentelli's article, 'Meaning and function of Kabyle ceramics' (p. 126), stopping when you reach the beginning of the section headed 'Changing techniques and meanings' on p. 133. Continue taking notes which summarise the content of the article. Note down which of the explanations of the function and decoration rely on the ethnographic approach of observing the objects in their original context or interviewing the people who first used the objects.

You should allow about 40 minutes for this activity.

Discussion

The function of the pots seems to be quite a flexible concept. At a basic level the function (whether for serving food or storing water) is related to the physical shape (in other words, the form) of the vessels. Some specialised items such as oil lamps have taken on ritual or ceremonial functions in addition to their original function of providing light. However, the ceramics are also said to have a function of representing social or cultural identity through their specific form and individual decoration. It may be possible to discern the basic function of a pot from its shape, but an understanding of the other various layers of functionality that the pots can perform seems to be something that can only really be reached by observing them in use or by interviewing the potters or users of the vessels. The suggestion that the pots are now primarily decorative (p. 127) introduces yet another possible function; it is something that might be suspected, but is only really verifiable by quizzing an informant.

Vincentelli's attempts to discover the meaning of the decoration seem to have been frustrated by her Kabyle informants, who provided replies that were not always 'clear or consistent' (p. 128). Explanations reported by other researchers were not entirely helpful either: it was said that the decoration was themed 'to amuse the clientele' (p. 130), for example, or that the purpose of the decoration was 'so that the chickens grow fat' (p. 130). Her own observation that the 'names of the motifs could change from one time to another and between different potters' (p. 130) adds to the challenge of interpreting the motifs. These emic explanations perhaps suggest that the Kabyle people may not conceive of decoration as having 'meaning' in the same way as an ethnographic researcher might.

Vincentelli also discusses explanations devised by other researchers, some of which appear to be derived from ethnographic studies of the Berbers, for example those relating the decoration to the 'evil eye' (p. 130) or unknown 'female magical practices' (p. 129). These ideas could be relevant to interpreting the motifs in the decoration, but there is little discussion of why the Kabyle might represent such things on their pottery. Nor are any emic viewpoints provided that could lend support to these suggestions, or to the roles of the different genders in Berber society.

The quotation (p. 129) from the influential anthropologist Pierre Bourdieu provides a structuralist explanation of how social structures unconsciously shape the decoration, and so the motifs can be related to divisions between public and private social activities and female and male gender identities. This explanation combines etic ideas about how social structure can influence behaviour with emic interpretations of the graphic symbols.

At the end of this section Vincentelli seeks an emic viewpoint on the 'aesthetic satisfaction' the women derive from creating the pottery (pp. 132–3). The two responses she cites are very different, illustrating the fact that the pots also have a personal context, since they are made and used by individuals, each of whom will have different motivations, inspirations and understandings. This observation is a warning that there is no single 'emic' viewpoint that might be discovered and also that one individual's viewpoint may not be representative of a society as a whole.

Vincentelli's investigations do not result in a conclusive discovery of 'the meaning' of the pots, but they do explore different ways of interpreting the pots within their context. It may feel disappointing that no firm conclusions about the meaning of the decoration on the pottery were found, but what emerges is that different meanings may coexist, depending on the viewpoint taken and the context within which the pottery is being interpreted.

The ethnographic approach has provided a detailed and layered understanding of the first stages of the life cycle of the pots. The ethnographic observations of the people and the society that created the Kabyle ceramics were made in the 1980s. However, it is worth remembering that the very similar vases in the Victoria and Albert Museum were acquired in 1868, and Kabyle society will have changed since that period, perhaps significantly. This suggests that the viewpoints of contemporary Kabyle people may not be entirely pertinent when we come to study 150-year-old pots. Nevertheless, the ceramics illustrated in the article are very similar to those in the museum – and even if Vincentelli draws attention to how different villages and individual women produce different styles of decoration, certain elements (the colours and shapes of vases, the general scheme of decoration, the appearance of the details of the decoration) appear little changed over a hundred years. Vincentelli's article goes on to discuss aspects of how the traditions are changing in recent times. Feel free to read this if you have the time to do so.

3.2 The archaeological approach

Taking the ethnographic approach to finding out about material culture and its context at the time of its production and first use works well when it is possible to identify the contemporary society that produced the items or, failing that, 'living relatives' preserving earlier traditions and technologies. Going back further in time makes the ethnographic approach more difficult. Is it safe to assume that the contemporary Kabyle are a reliable source of information about life in Algeria 500 years ago? Is there any evidence to suggest that their way of life has remained unchanged for half a millennium? Going back even further, we might imagine that interrogating modern Italians to discover the context of ancient Roman artefacts would not be of much help. To understand about ancient objects we need to use different historical and archaeological methodologies. It also becomes necessary to accept that our knowledge of the past will always be imperfect and we shall be able to achieve only a partial reconstruction of ancient contexts. Archaeology typically deals with broken artefacts and ruined buildings, and so we can expect to find only incomplete contexts.

Archaeological context

In archaeology the term 'context' has both a specific and a more general meaning. It is used to mean an archaeological layer distinct from surrounding layers. An archaeological layer comprises the identifiable physical remains of some action in the past. Its colour, consistency or constituents might distinguish it from surrounding layers. For example, the remains of a bucket full of Roman rubbish thrown into a pit dug into a chalky subsoil could survive as a layer of dark earth rich in organic material, full of animal bones and broken crockery, distinct from the surrounding white chalky rock. The 'context' of one of those pieces of broken crockery refers to all the other material – earth and other objects – that it was found with. The term 'assemblage' is often used to denote all of the artefacts found in a single context.

If an object becomes separated from the other things it was deposited with it is said to be 'without context', or 'out of context', meaning that it is not known where or when it was found or what it was found with. This creates a serious problem, limiting the description, understanding and interpretation of an object to its intrinsic qualities alone (see Figure 3.3).

More generally, 'context' also means the location and circumstances where something was either found or originally produced or used. So the context of a piece of broken crockery could also be the archaeological site and geographical location where it was excavated, or the ancient context of the Roman house that produced the rubbish and also functioned within the context of Roman society and culture.

Figure 3.3 Bracelets, rings, pins, mirrors and other jewellery from nineteenth-century excavations in Pompeii – but displayed out of context. National Archaeological Museum, Naples. Photo: © Alinari Archives – Brogi Archive, Florence

For the remainder of this chapter, you will be studying an archaeological context. It is a very remarkable one that was created in extraordinary circumstances: the buried city of Pompeii.

Pompeii: creation of a context

The city of Pompeii, 20 kilometres (12.5 miles) to the southeast of Naples in Italy, was destroyed in the volcanic eruption of Mount Vesuvius in the year 79 CE. The remains of the ancient city were buried by over 5 metres of volcanic deposits that were ejected from the volcano. The fumes, ashes, stones (*lapilli* in Latin) and heat killed many people, burying them under a layer of ash and stone. The weight of the ashes and the strength of the earth tremors caused buildings to collapse. They, too, were buried in ashes, so sealing beneath them objects that became incorporated in archaeological layers. In this way, human remains and artefacts in use at the time of the eruption were preserved and protected from later damage. Pompeii is a very special place because of the way the remains were buried and have been preserved. We are also very lucky that a text has survived that is an eyewitness account of the destruction of the city and the creation of the archaeological site.

Activity

You should allow about 20 minutes for this activity.

Pliny the Younger (*c*.61–*c*.112 CE) was a Roman author whose output included many letters to other important Roman citizens. (If you have studied AA100 *The arts past and present*, you might remember reading some extracts from Pliny's letters as part of your study of Book 4, Chapter 3.) At the end of this chapter you will find Reading 3.1, which reprints a letter written by him to the historian Suetonius (*c*.71–*c*.135 CE), describing the eruption of Vesuvius and the death of his uncle, Pliny the Elder (23–79 CE). You should read the letter now. As you read, look out for items of material culture and also the processes that could have led to these being preserved in the archaeological record.

Discussion

Pliny the Younger's narrative describes the eruption as seen from afar and then moves on to tell of the death of his uncle (a story presumably told to him by survivors) at Stabiae, a harbour town near to Pompeii. As Pliny the Elder snored, the courtyard of the house where he was staying was gradually filling with 'ashes mixed with pumice-stones'. The account also tells us that 'buildings were now shaking with violent shocks, and seemed to be swaying to and fro as if they were torn from their foundations', indicating the devastation to come. This is an eyewitness account of the process that led to the partial burial and preservation of Pompeii.

The fires seen on the mountainside – if created by houses burning down – would have caused archaeological layers to be formed as the houses and their contents were burned. However, it would seem more likely that the 'fires' were molten lava, and that Pliny the Elder was trying to reassure his companions by suggesting otherwise.

Pliny the Younger's account provides a dramatic image of the destruction and suffering caused by the volcano, but his narrative is not simply a documentary account. It is just as much a tale of how his uncle died a heroic death and how the younger Pliny seeks to perpetuate his memory by having the episode written into history (Jones, 2001).

Nevertheless, Pliny does incidentally mention quite a few material things. These are the items of material culture mentioned in the extract that I noted:

- cities
- people
- books
- fleet
- shoes
- boat
- message
- house
- warships
- belongings
- bathroom
- door
- room
- courtyard
- buildings
- foundations
- pillows
- cloths
- torches
- lamps
- sheet
- clothes.

The first item, 'cities', is, perhaps, stretching the idea of material culture, but the built environment is in essence something that is designed, constructed and used by people, and it even has a life cycle, so it may therefore be included as a part of material culture. Many of the other material items in the extract are also related to the built environment: a house, a bathroom, a door, a room, a courtyard, buildings and foundations. Pliny does not describe them in detail, but they all add up to form the setting for the story and are therefore also the kind of items that would make up the context for any archaeological finds beneath the ashes of the volcano. All the items sound familiar and create a domestic setting that it is possible to relate to but, as you will shortly discover, the Roman versions of these homely items were not all like contemporary objects. Apart from the buildings, the individual objects are all of a domestic nature: books, shoes, 'belongings', pillows, cloths, torches, lamps, sheet and clothes. To some extent, Pliny's decision to include these domestic items in his narrative helps the reader to relate to the everyday setting of the tragedy and to empathise with the victims. In contrast to the built environment, many of these items are made of perishable materials and are only ever preserved in archaeological contexts in exceptional conditions, such as the eruption of Mount Vesuvius.

One possible material item is the message that Pliny receives from Rectina, asking for rescue. The extract uses the word 'message', which could signify an oral message, but the original Latin word used is *codicillos*, meaning 'a note', so that suggests it was actually a written message and so would have been a material object, perhaps a wax tablet with the message inscribed on its surface. The remaining things are a boat and the fleet, which once again are built objects used by people.

Finally there are 'people' themselves, the victims of the natural disaster. Now you might quite reasonably complain that these are *people* and not objects of material culture, but where can the boundary be drawn? Consider, for example, bodily modifications such as tattoos, piercings or cosmetic surgery. Is this making the body into an artefact? Does modifying the body to send cultural messages transform it into material culture? Or, to take another example, what about an Egyptian mummy in a museum? It is an embalmed and embellished selection of bodily remains creating something that is part human body yet part artefact; something that was first in an assemblage of items in a tomb and then an exhibit in a museum collection. Has it become material culture as it progresses through its life cycle? At Pompeii, traces of bodies were preserved under the ashes as 'voids' (where the ash settled over a body that subsequently decomposed, this preserved an empty space, or void, like a fossil imprint of the body). Excavators finding these voids filled them with plaster or resin as if they were moulds, thereby recreating the form of the body. Many of these body casts are displayed at Pompeii and form a unique part of the archaeological context there.

However, at Pompeii it was not the case that everything was 'frozen' in an instant. As you have read, some people had a chance to escape. Pomponianus, for instance, had 'put his belongings on board ship', and people's attempts to escape or hide from the ashes and stones mean that things would not necessarily have been in their normal positions when buried by the ashes. Furthermore, after the eruption attempts were made to salvage objects from the ruined city and many of the buildings have been disturbed by digging and tunnelling, from the Roman period onwards.

In more recent times, excavations began in the mid eighteenth century and in 1763 an inscription was found that identified the archaeological remains as the city of Pompeii. Excavations have continued at the site since then, but before the twentieth century records of what was found, and where it was found, were poorly kept, so many objects found in Pompeii are without a detailed context. In effect, much archaeological information was not recorded. Therefore it is not always possible to accurately relate objects now in museums to where they were found and so fully interpret ancient Roman activities and lifestyles.

Pompeii may not simply be a fossilised Roman city, but the degree of its preservation is remarkable. Despite the destruction, many items have been found which were last used in 79 CE, in some cases along with the remains of the people who used them. Because of this, at Pompeii it is possible to study individual contexts and their associated assemblages of objects alongside the people themselves. This makes it possible to study the world of objects used by people in the Roman city and what they can tell us about Roman society.

People and all their things: the House of Menander

Pompeii was a city that extended over 66 hectares (163 acres), enclosed by 3.5 kilometres (2 miles) of city walls and divided into city blocks by paved streets (see Figure 3.4). Each city block contained several houses. Each house was entered from the street through a passage that ran between shops or rooms on the street front. The grander houses were usually arranged around a small courtyard (**atrium**) (see Figure 3.5) and a garden space (**peristyle**). Shortly, you will be studying one of these houses in the southern part of the city: the House of Menander (see Figure 3.6). This house is named after the Greek playwright Menander, who lived from the fourth to the third centuries BCE, because his portrait was painted on a wall in the garden of the house, not because

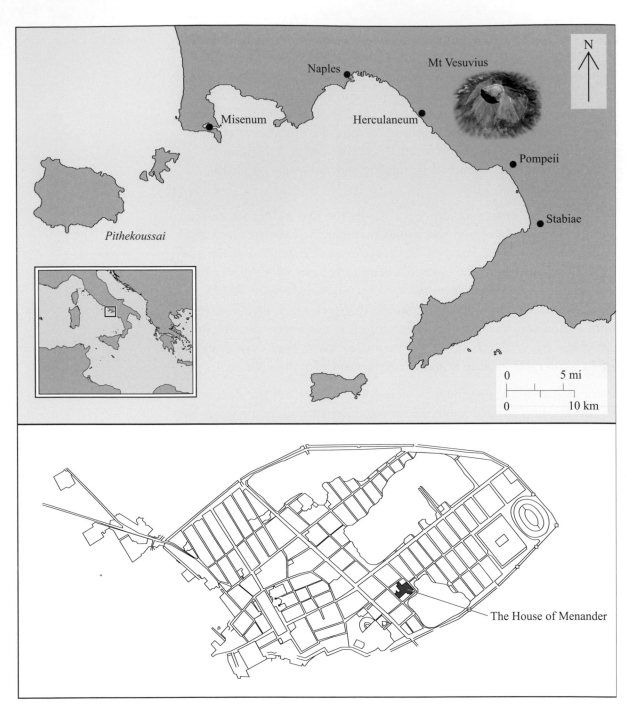

Figure 3.4 Street plan of Pompeii, showing the location of the House of Menander, and map of surrounding area

Figure 3.5 Atrium of the House of Menander, Pompeii. Photographed by Fratelli Alinari, 1935. Photo: © Alinari Archives – Alinari Archive, Florence

he lived there; the name of the actual owner is not known. The house has been chosen for study because it is well preserved and has been meticulously investigated; many details of the structure and decoration have been researched (Allison, 2006; Ling, 1996; Maiuri, 1932). Additionally, all of the objects found in the house have been studied, meaning that it is possible to study the entire assemblage. Altogether, 2436 items excavated from the house in the 1920s have been catalogued.

At the time of the eruption the house appears not to have been fully occupied. There had been an earthquake in Pompeii in 62 CE and 17 years later, when Vesuvius erupted, many buildings were still being restored and repaired. The House of Menander seems to have been nearly fully repaired but not yet wholly in use. Therefore, its almost 2500 items represent only a fraction of the complete range of material culture that a fully functioning large Roman house would have contained. You will be studying the whole house first, to gain an impression of how a Roman house was organised and the general form

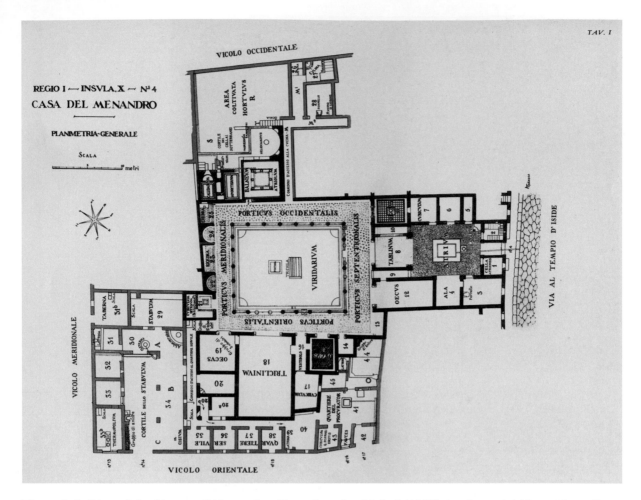

Figure 3.6 Plan of the House of Menander. From Amedeo Maiuri (1932) *La Casa del Menandro e il suo Tesoro di Argenteria*, vol. 2, Rome, Libreria dello Stato

of the built environment and decoration that form a part of this material culture. Then you will be focusing on a small suite of rooms in the eastern part of the house, known as the 'procurator's quarters', that appears to have been occupied at the time of eruption, studying all of the items found in those rooms – a more manageable total of 395 items (see Figures 3.7–3.9).

Activity

You should allow about an hour for this activity.

You should now complete the online activity 'The House of Menander', which you can find on the Study Planner of the module website. In this activity, you will encounter plans and images of the House of Menander, along with a database of its contents.

Figure 3.7 Atrium of the 'procurator's quarters', Room 41 of the House of Menander, Pompeii. Photographed by Fratelli Alinari, 1935. Photo: © Alinari Archives – Alinari Archive, Florence

Figure 3.8 Courtyard of the 'procurator's quarters', Room 44 of the House of Menander, looking east. From Amedeo Maiuri (1932) *La Casa del Menandro e il suo Tesoro di Argenteria*, vol. 2, Rome, Libreria dello Stato

context(s) that have now been excavated. Each has a biography that extends over thousands of years, although some parts of this biography may be more tangible than others (those parts that coincide with the eruption, for instance, or their current location in the museum).

Conclusion

In this chapter you have studied a range of objects from very different contexts. The Kabyle ceramics began their lives about 150 years ago and people in contemporary Algeria would still recognise the vases as belonging to their material culture. This enables an ethnographic approach, where objects can be observed in use and the people who use them can be asked about these objects and their uses and any meaning they may have. Aspects of the object life cycle encountered here focus on the production and consumption phases. You have seen that the ethnographic approach can provide insights into material culture, but it does not necessarily provide clear answers to questions that outsiders might ask about the objects that they observe.

In the second part of the chapter you studied a very well-preserved archaeological context in Pompeii. The objects found here are in the afterlife phase of their life cycles. Here it is not possible to ask the people themselves what went on, or what they thought about the objects they used. This required an archaeological approach, which works from the objects themselves and their contexts. It attempts to reconstruct past lives and attitudes through interpreting surviving objects and their contexts. Inevitably a perfect reconstruction is not possible, because the evidence is fragmentary, but the objects that people used can reveal many aspects of their lives and circumstances. In both case studies, the questions to be answered concern the lives of the objects *before* they reached the glass case of the museum display, with the reminder that the museum case may not be the first context for an object's afterlife.

References

Allison, P.M. (2006) *The Insula of the Menander at Pompeii*, volume 3: *The Finds: A Contextual Study*, Oxford, Clarendon Press.

Jones, N.F. (2001) 'Pliny the Younger's Vesuvius "Letters" (6.16 and 6.20)', *The Classical World*, vol. 95, no. 1, pp. 31–48.

Ling, R. (ed.) (1996) *The Insula of the Menander at Pompeii*, volume 1: *The Structures*, Oxford, Clarendon Press.

Maiuri, A. (1932) *La Casa del Menandro e il suo Tesoro di Argenteria*, 2 vols, Rome, Libreria dello Stato.

Radice, B. (trans.) (1969) *The Letters of the Younger Pliny*, Harmondsworth, Penguin.

Vincentelli, M. (1989) 'Reflections on a Kabyle pot: Algerian women and the decorative tradition', *Journal of Design History*, vol. 2, nos 2/3, pp. 123–38.

Further reading

There are a huge number of publications on Pompeii that range from specialist reports to general guidebooks. Two reliable and engaging books are Mary Beard (2009) and Joanne Berry (2007).

Specific publications on the House of Menander are harder to find, but, in addition to those in the References, Grete Stefani's edited work (2003) is a beautifully illustrated publication in Italian.

For the Berbers, the best history in English is Michael Brett and Elizabeth Fentress (1997). For a more contemporary perspective, there is Karen E. Hoffman and Susan G. Miller's (2010) collection of essays.

You might also want to look up the objects shown in Figures 3.1 and 3.2 on the Victoria and Albert museum website.

Beard, M. (2009) *Pompeii: The Life of a Roman Town*, London, Profile Books.

Berry, J. (2007) *The Complete Pompeii*, London, Thames & Hudson.

Brett, M. and Fentress, E. (1997) *Berbers (Peoples of Africa)*, Oxford, Wiley-Blackwell.

Hoffman, K.E. and Miller, S.G. (2010) *Berbers and Others: Beyond Tribe and Nation in the Maghrib*, Bloomington and Indianapolis, IN, Indiana University Press.

Stefani, G. (ed.) (2003) *Menander la Casa del Menandro di Pompei*, Milan, Electa.

Reading 3.1   The eruption of Vesuvius

Source: Radice, B. (trans.) (1969) *The Letters of the Younger Pliny*, Harmondsworth, Penguin, pp. 166–8.

Thank you for asking me to send you a description of my uncle's death so that you can leave an accurate account of it for posterity; I know that immortal fame awaits him if his death is recorded by you. It is true that he perished in a catastrophe which destroyed the loveliest regions of the earth, a fate shared by whole cities and their people, and one so memorable that it is likely to make his name live for ever; and he himself wrote a number of books of lasting value: but you write for all time and can still do much to perpetuate his memory. The fortunate man, in my opinion, is he to whom the gods have granted the power either to do something which is worth recording or to write what is worth reading, and most fortunate of all is the man who can do both. Such a man was my uncle, as his own books and yours will prove. So you set me a task I would choose for myself, and I am more than willing to start on it.

Misenum is the northern arm of the bay of Naples (now Capo Miseno).

My uncle was stationed at Misenum, in active command of the fleet. On 24 August, in the early afternoon, my mother drew his attention to a cloud of unusual size and appearance. He had been out in the sun, had taken a cold bath, and lunched while lying down, and was then working at his books. He called for his shoes and climbed up to a place which would give him the best view of the phenomenon. It was not clear at that distance from which mountain the cloud was rising (it was afterwards known to be Vesuvius); its general appearance can best be expressed as being like an umbrella pine, for it rose to a great height on a sort of trunk and then split off into branches, I imagine because it was thrust upwards by the first blast and then left unsupported as the pressure subsided, or else it was borne down by its own weight so that it spread out and gradually dispersed. Sometimes it looked white, sometimes blotched and dirty, according to the amount of soil and ashes it carried with it. My uncle's scholarly acumen saw at once that it was important enough for a closer inspection, and he ordered a boat to be made ready, telling me I could come with him if I wished. I replied that I preferred to go on with my studies, and as it happened he had himself given me some writing to do.

As he was leaving the house he was handed a message from Rectina, wife of Tascus whose house was at the foot of the mountain, so that escape was impossible except by boat. She was terrified by the danger threatening her and implored him to rescue her from her fate. He changed his plans, and what he had begun in a spirit of inquiry he completed as a hero. He gave orders for the warships to be launched and went on board himself with the intention of bringing help to many more people besides Rectina, for this lovely stretch of coast was thickly populated. He hurried to the place which everyone else was hastily leaving, steering his course straight for the danger zone. He was entirely fearless, describing each new movement and phase of the portent to be noted down exactly as he observed them. Ashes were already falling, hotter and thicker as the ships drew near, followed by bits of pumice and blackened stones, charred and cracked by the flames: then suddenly they were in shallow water, and the shore was blocked by the debris from the mountain. For a moment my uncle wondered whether to turn back, but when the helmsman advised this he refused, telling him that Fortune stood by the courageous and they must make for Pomponianus at Stabiae. He was cut off there by the breadth of the bay (for the shore gradually curves round a basin filled by the sea) so that he was not as yet in danger, though it was clear that this would come nearer as it spread. Pomponianus had therefore already put his belongings on board ship, intending to escape if the contrary wind fell. This wind was of course full in my uncle's favour, and he was able to bring his ship in. He embraced his terrified friend, cheered and encouraged him, and thinking he could calm his fears by showing his own composure, gave orders that he was to be carried to the bathroom. After his bath he lay down and dined; he was quite cheerful, or at any rate he pretended he was, which was no less courageous.

Stabiae is four miles [6.5 km] south of Pompeii.

Meanwhile on Mount Vesuvius broad sheets of fire and leaping flames blazed at several points, their bright glare emphasized by the darkness of night. My uncle tried to allay the fears of his companions by repeatedly declaring that these were nothing but bonfires left by the peasants in their terror, or else empty houses on fire in the districts they had abandoned. Then he went to rest and certainly slept, for as he was a stout man his breathing was rather loud and heavy and could be heard by people coming and going outside his door. By this time the courtyard giving access to his room was full of ashes mixed with pumice-stones, so that its level had risen, and if he had stayed in the room any longer he would never have got out. He was wakened, came out and joined Pomponianus and the rest of the household who had sat up all night. They debated whether to stay indoors or take their chance in the open, for the buildings were now shaking with violent shocks,

Contents

Aims

This chapter will:

- introduce you to how books can be understood as objects
- develop your ability to interpret aspects of print
- explore the contexts of the European printing revolution
- develop your skills in using key information resources.

Materials you will need

In this chapter, you will need to watch the following films, which can be found on the module website:

- The handpress in action
- Anatomy of a book.

You will also be directed to the website for an online activity.

Introduction

For people who think of themselves as readers, books are everyday objects. The relationship between the object and the user is the crucial stimulus that brings a book to life – consider the expression used when someone feels shut out from a subject: 'This is a closed book to me.' This chapter develops your understanding of contexts by using the historical contexts around how printed books were pioneered, designed, used and thought about in England. It looks at the standard process of production for the period 1450–1800, and explores how books could be used and appreciated as objects as well as bearers of the printed word.

Although this chapter is produced for a printed book, you might be reading it on a computer screen or as an ebook on a tablet computer. You may be familiar with other ways of reading a text. In recent years, digital formats for books (ebooks) have become increasingly popular. The Open University Library subscribes to a wide range of ebooks and ejournals created by academic publishers. Some of these formats allow you to interact with the electronic text, by annotating or highlighting it, as you might with pen on paper. And in the connected digital world you can share and view other people's annotations. Historians who are interested in what readers thought about texts search historic books for annotations, as you will see later in the chapter.

A book is intended to carry some text, with or without illustrations, and most of us use books, printed or digital, as a means of supplying us with some information or for leisure. However, the physical form of books has long been a subject of research: as with any object, the form of the book has a history (it has changed shape over thousands of years of literacy) and a community of scholars who investigate it. Practitioners of several academic disciplines come together in researching the book as an object: literary scholars, art historians, social and cultural historians, who may be based in university departments, or work as professional librarians or museum curators. They are interested in the structure of books, including paper, bindings and ink types; in the people and processes involved in making and selling books; and in readers and collectors, some of whom leave traces of their reading habits on the books that pass through their hands. Collectively, this research is known as book history (or history of the book).

My own interest as an architectural historian begins with a place for reading and keeping books: the library and its contents. The Open

University hosts a massive online database called the Reading Experience Database (RED), which collects evidence for reading in Britain between 1450 and 1945. This database collects evidence on where texts (not just those in books) were read, and by whom, as well as on what readers thought about the texts. These are examples of contexts for the practice of reading, similar to the contexts for where a pot was made and by whom. The nature of the evidence in the RED is historical rather than ethnographic or archaeological, since the evidence comes from written sources. The start date for the database is also the beginning of this chapter.

The chapter explores the early centuries of the printed book in western culture, from about 1450 to 1800. This is the era of the **handpress**: the early printing press, operated by human muscle power. First demonstrated in Germany in 1455, the technology was rapidly adopted as presses were set up in a number of European towns (see Figure 4.1) by pioneer printers/publishers such as Johannes Gutenberg and William Caxton (discussed below). Almost six centuries later, printing remains a success story – which is why it is the chosen media for delivering the content of this chapter. Its success was so rapid that this process has been characterised as a **printing revolution**: it was revolutionary in the way it made information accessible, and in the social, political and economic shifts that it created and that can be seen to underpin the modern world.

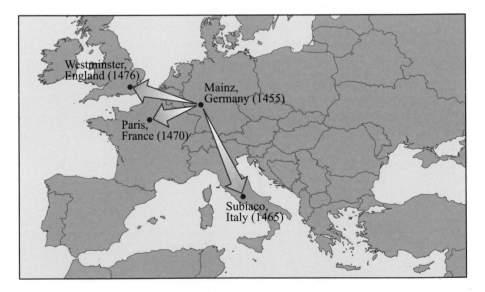

Figure 4.1 Map showing the locations of early European printing presses

Traditional printing is, as noted earlier, no longer the only medium for disseminating information. The words in this chapter have been written on a laptop computer, and alternative ways of reading them involve opening up a computer file and seeing them as pixels on a monitor, or printing them on demand on loose sheets of paper. Students and researchers in the fields of arts and humanities today can spend more time on searching and reading computer files of text than they might spend on reading printed and bound books. Since the development of personal computers from the 1970s onwards, and the invention of the world wide web in 1989, another information revolution has been identified: the digital revolution (often also called the 'virtual revolution'), which refers to the range of human activity that is now conducted using digital technology. In 2012, over 78 per cent of the population of North America used the internet, along with 63 per cent of those in Europe, but only 15 per cent of people in Africa. (Notice how the source for these statistics is itself a webpage: see Internet World Stats, Usage and Population Statistics, 2014.) There are big inequalities of age and socio-economic background (less so of gender) among those who do or do not have internet access. Such access also presumes literacy, which is still not universal. Cultural and technological revolutions, then, may not be experienced by all individuals, but they do signify shifts in the ways in which culture is produced and transmitted.

The early interactions between books and readers shaped both the organisation and content of printed books and the ways in which readers made connections between books. Early 'hyperlinks' were systems of intellectual cross-references, scribbled in margins, catalogued in lists, or argued over in letters to other readers.

The differences in the material form and organisation of early printed books (those produced, roughly speaking, between about 1450 and about 1800), compared with those produced today, are increasingly understood by literary and book historians to make a difference to the experiences of both writers and readers then and now. Today, few people read their favourite eighteenth- or nineteenth-century novels in the historic first editions – the novels I own by Jane Austen (1775– 1817) are all cheap paperbacks printed in the last 20 years. One physical book equals one complete text. When, out of curiosity to see what it looked like, I ordered up the oldest copy of Austen's *Pride and Prejudice* in my university library, I was handed not one but three little volumes published in 1813 (the second edition). These were about paperback height – 18cm – but the text was printed on thicker, slightly rougher paper than would be the case today, and it was laid out very differently (see Figure 4.2). At the bottom of each page, I found that the first word of the next page was reproduced. My reading speed slowed down as the unfamiliar design of the typeface and the layout took more time to assimilate. I felt as though I needed to practise how to read: an experience I had not expected. Austen's novels were written and published right at the end of the period covered by this chapter.

This chapter discusses the early modern book as an object that has a life cycle, beginning with its inception as an intellectual concept (the author's manuscript) and proceeding until it is given material form as a printed and bound volume. The book then goes out into the social world to be read, shelved, reread and perhaps sold on (even destroyed or cut up for its illustrations). All of these life stages leave marks. Individual books also show unique features that are part of their biography, to a degree that may be surprising compared with your experience of mass-printed modern books.

David Pearson, a leading scholar in the field of historic book bindings, points out that we have many means of access to historic texts in our current digital age, as the result of huge investment in digitising historic printed works as online collections, as well as decades of cheap print editions. The historic books themselves, stored in national and university libraries and specialist study collections, have not been superseded, however. 'What remains unique in all these collections is not the texts, but the books as artefacts, whose bindings and other copy-specific characteristics are an irreplaceable part of our historic fabric' (Pearson, 2005, p. viii).

A final point to consider is that books acquire all sorts of uses beyond carrying text to be read. Early printed books were produced when paper was handmade and relatively costly, and blank sheets at the front and back of a book could be useful for handwriting practice or for jotting down quite unrelated notes or lists. Books could also take on some special powers by virtue of the authority of the texts they contained, particularly religious texts. Courts in England still, at the time of writing, require witnesses either to swear a religious oath on a holy book or to make an affirmation without religious content: notice how the oath is not complete without the holy book. These varied functions and symbolic meanings of books are further examples of how an object shifts in meaning as the contexts of its use and display change.

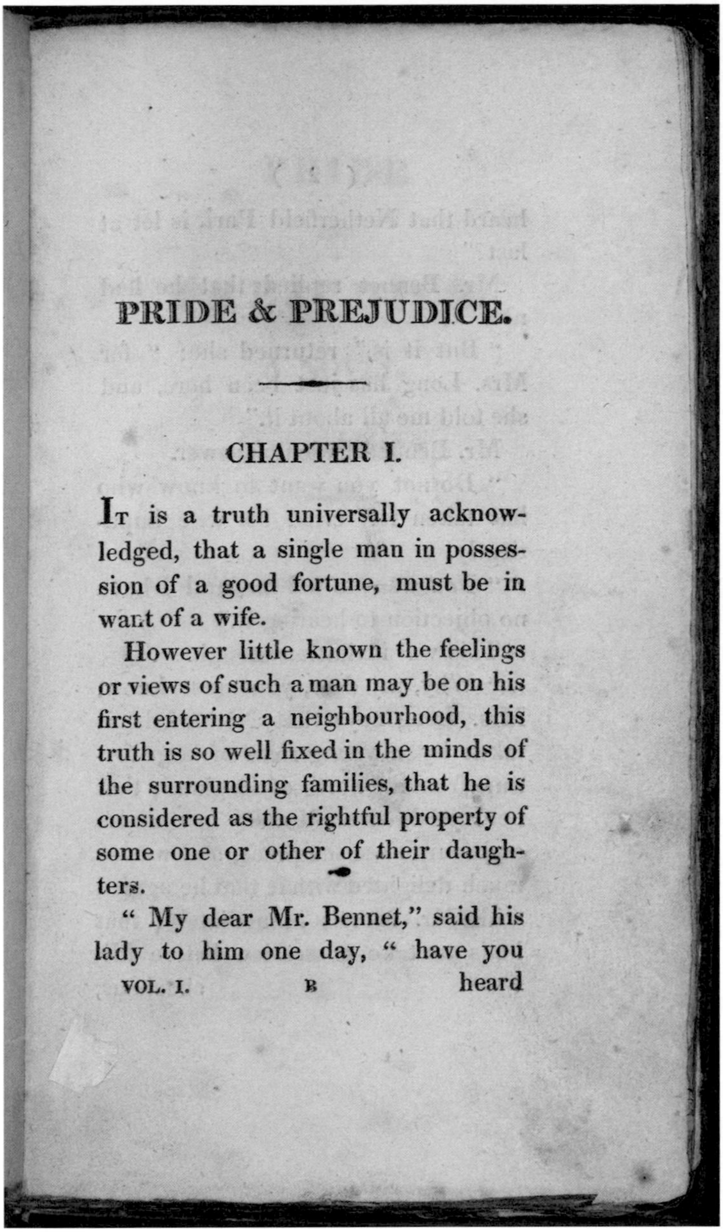

PRIDE & PREJUDICE.

CHAPTER I.

It is a truth universally acknowledged, that a single man in possession of a good fortune, must be in want of a wife.

However little known the feelings or views of such a man may be on his first entering a neighbourhood, this truth is so well fixed in the minds of the surrounding families, that he is considered as the rightful property of some one or other of their daughters.

" My dear Mr. Bennet," said his lady to him one day, " have you

VOL. I. B heard

Figure 4.2 The opening page of Chapter 1 of Jane Austen (1813) *Pride and Prejudice*. Published by T. Egerton, London. British Library, London, 1650/20. Photo: © The British Library Board

4.1 Taking a book apart

What can you do with this book? It is an activity zone in your hands. Here is a quick exercise to make this book seem less taken for granted as an object.

Activity

You should allow about 10 minutes for this activity.

Think back to the first time you held this book. Close it up and reconstruct your actions. Become aware of how you handle the object, and what you are looking for.

What do you take for granted about this object?

Discussion

When I pick up a new book, I become aware of the texture of the cover and the weight of the volume, which tells me something about the nature of the materials used and their apparent quality. Once I have scanned the front cover for information (what do I understand from the title? Do I recognise the author?), I usually turn the book over to scan the back cover for extra clues (are there endorsements from other readers printed here?). Then it is time to open the front cover, skimming past the early pages to find the contents page, where I see chapter titles listed. If there is a chapter heading that particularly interests me, I can find the page number noted beside it and dip into the text. I can also hold the book half-closed and quickly flip the pages to see if there are illustrations, and how they are scattered through the book. I am barely aware of the sound of the crisp new paper being moved, or of the scent of the newly revealed paper and ink.

I take for granted that this book, written in my own language, can be read sequentially from front to back, that there are navigation aids (a contents page, page numbers, an index at the back), that it has a protective cover and that it is designed for the level of use expected of it.

The twenty-first century book, a product of modern publishing practices, is highly standardised. Its features reflect the interests of the intended reader, and also those of the publisher, the book trade and the library sector: people who need to distribute, circulate, store and retrieve the book. Features that a reader can ignore, such as a bar code (Universal Product Code) and the data on the back of the title page about international standard book numbers and cataloguing data, place the modern book within a global network of shared information standards. The bar code is one example of a printed design that has come to have a standardised position on the back cover. It instantly links the book as an object to the digital revolution.

Before printing mechanised this delivery, handwritten (or manuscript) books were the only means of producing multiple copies of a text. Such handwritten and handmade books are familiar as some of the treasures of western medieval Europe, particularly gorgeously designed and coloured religious texts such as bibles and prayer-books. We tend to view these as unique, but, in practice, scribes working in groups could produce multiple copies of handwritten texts for widespread distribution. Handwriting as a technology for reproduction does not of itself limit the transmission of knowledge.

Everything we see in a book has a history in terms of its material form, whose origins might be quite different from its current (and perhaps therefore not final) appearance. Many of the printed features that help you to move around a book can be described as **metadata**. Title pages, contents lists, indexes, chapter headings, and the like sit above the data contained in the text and act as guides or descriptors of that text (literary scholars prefer to call this 'extra' text **paratext**: a term coined by the French literary theorist Gérard Genette (1997 [1987]). Without metadata, the text can be read and understood, but it becomes harder to navigate around – and it becomes even harder to think of quick ways of comparing it with other texts. A library catalogue (which is itself a database) is a collection of metadata: author and title are the building blocks of the catalogue and are selected in order to 'describe' the text.

The material form that the text takes is important in terms of how data and metadata can be presented within it. Historians of the book now tend to distinguish between the intellectual content of a text – 'the work' – and the physical delivery of the work as a text for reading – 'the text' (Chartier, 1994 [1992]; Tanselle, 1989). 'The work' could be experienced in different forms, as a tangible text, or intangibly as a live theatrical performance or a radio broadcast. The physical text is a material means for transmitting the work from one reader to another reader or listener. Texts can take a variety of forms, from single leaves made of bamboo (such as early Buddhist texts), to ancient Roman wax tablets, to scrolls made of plant-based material (such as papyrus) or animal skin. The Romans went on to invent the form of the book you are holding today: a form called the **codex**. This word describes a book made up of folded **parchment** (prepared animal skin), stitched together along a fold. The codex emerged in the first century CE and it has not been superseded as a physical form. A codex can be a manuscript or a printed book. It does not have to have a protective binding.

The codex is a success because this form makes it easy to multiply pages in order to suit the length of the work (or the works collected together) and still keep them in a convenient single block. If you close this book and hold it vertically to see the top edge of the pages, you will notice that where the pages meet the cover they are grouped into sections, one or two millimetres thick. These sections of folded pages are called **gatherings**. Modern binding uses glue to keep the gatherings together, instead of fabric stitches. But the final form of the gatherings comes only after the edges have been trimmed by a knife. This creates an illusion that modern books are printed on paper that is folded only once.

This brings us to the second reason for the success of the codex as the medium for print. A large piece of paper can be printed with eight or more pages-worth of text on each side, which is an efficient use of the printing press. A single sheet can be folded several times after it has been printed. So long as the printer sets up individual pages of text in the right position on the press, then, when folded in the correct order, three of the folded edges can be cut and the fourth edge becomes the fold for glueing or stitching.

If the Romans invented the codex form, why did it take Europe over 1000 years after the fall of the Roman empire for printing to take over from manuscript copying? The idea of printing was not new in western Europe: images carved on to blocks of wood, inked up and pressed directly on to a page, were already being used on the same page as handwritten text. (China had used woodblock printing since the 800s CE.) Mechanically reproduced text was the great breakthrough in fifteenth-century Europe, and this was made possible by the invention of metal type.

Activity

You should allow about 25 minutes for this activity.

You should now find the film 'The handpress in action' on the module website, which shows how a printer produces a printed sheet from a handpress. This film, drawn from the Open University film archive, was created in 1972 for one of the OU's first courses, *Renaissance and reformation*, which adopted a multidisciplinary approach to the fifteenth and sixteenth centuries in Europe. It is narrated by the Open University's first professor of History, Arthur Marwick. Shot in black and white, the film provides exceptional access to a master printer, shown using a reconstructed fifteenth-century handpress in the Gutenberg Museum in Mainz, Germany.

Watch this short film now and take brief notes to record each stage of the processes shown. How many stages can you identify?

Discussion

At the close of the film, we are told there are 12 single operations involved. Here are the steps that result in printed pages:

- Type-making: the design is created.
- Type-making: the mould matrix (negative impression) is created.
- Type-making: the type is cast.
- Composition: individual pieces of type are set up in lines of text.
- Composition: each line is transferred to a galley to fill each intended page.
- The press: the galley is fixed into a frame (or 'form', or 'chase') on the press.
- The press: the form, full of type, is inked.
- The press: the paper sheet is placed in a frame called the 'sledge'.
- The press: the sledge is pushed on to the press.
- The press: a wooden screw is turned by using a lever to press down on to the platen, or press bed.
- The press: the platen is raised, the bed slides out again, and the printed paper can be removed.
- The sheets: the printed paper is hung up to dry.

The voiceover refers to two of Gutenberg's printed books: the 42-line Bible and the Mainz psalter. The Mainz psalter is a prayer-book printed three years after the Gutenberg Bible and is the first printed book to use printed decoration. Only ten copies of the psalter survive – they are regarded as part of our global heritage, inscribed on UNESCO's 'Memory of the world register' in 2001 (UNESCO, 2014).

Typefaces are the designs for letters and other symbols that you see on this page, usually created as complete sets of letters, numbers, punctuation marks and other symbols (collectively called a **font**). Mechanical typewriters use the same principle of cast metal types, except that each type is attached to a lever. The European credited with the invention of movable type is Johannes Gutenberg (*c*.1394–1468).

Born into a wealthy family in the German city of Mainz, Gutenberg seems to have developed a specialist interest in metalworking to make luxury products, which may have helped him in thinking about devising individually cast pieces of type. (Recent research, however, suggests that Gutenberg's technique for making type was superseded by the work of his colleague Nicolas Jenson (1420–*c*.1480), who by 1459 had developed the resilient cast type required for busy workshops (Hellinga, 2007).) Gutenberg's knowledge of luxury goods was certainly important, since highly decorated manuscripts were, of course, owned only by the literate and wealthy in society. The success of his invention was initially because the new printing matched the quality of handwritten luxury manuscripts. It was not at first aimed at a mass market. This is demonstrated by Gutenberg's major project: the printing of a Bible, the largest and most significant Christian text, which was completed in 1455. He printed 135 copies on paper and 45 on **vellum**, a fine quality of parchment, bound as two volumes. Only 16 copies survive today (see Figure 4.3).

Notice how the pages of the paper version of Gutenberg's Bible closely follow the design conventions of contemporary manuscripts. The printed element is the black type, which uses a design that every scribe writing manuscripts used. Everything else, including the red text that starts the page, is added by hand. The high-quality results were a success, every copy was sold and Gutenberg quickly became famous.

The Gutenberg Bible was set up to print as two pages on each sheet – so when the sheet was printed on both sides, only one fold was necessary to put the pages into the correct sequence (the technical description of this treatment of the sheet is **folio**).

Activity

You should allow about 20 minutes for this activity.

To understand something of the complexity of getting pages of print the right way up and in the correct order, take a sheet of A4 paper. You will also need a pen and a pair of scissors. On one side of the paper, make some distinctive lines across all of it (I used cross-hatching) in order to recognise this side of the paper later. Now fold the paper in half (instinctively you will fold the long edge – so you will end up with a greetings card form: the folio). Next, fold this folio in half, and then in half once again (each time along the long edge). So you will have made three folds in all. You have created a little book – in fact this is one gathering

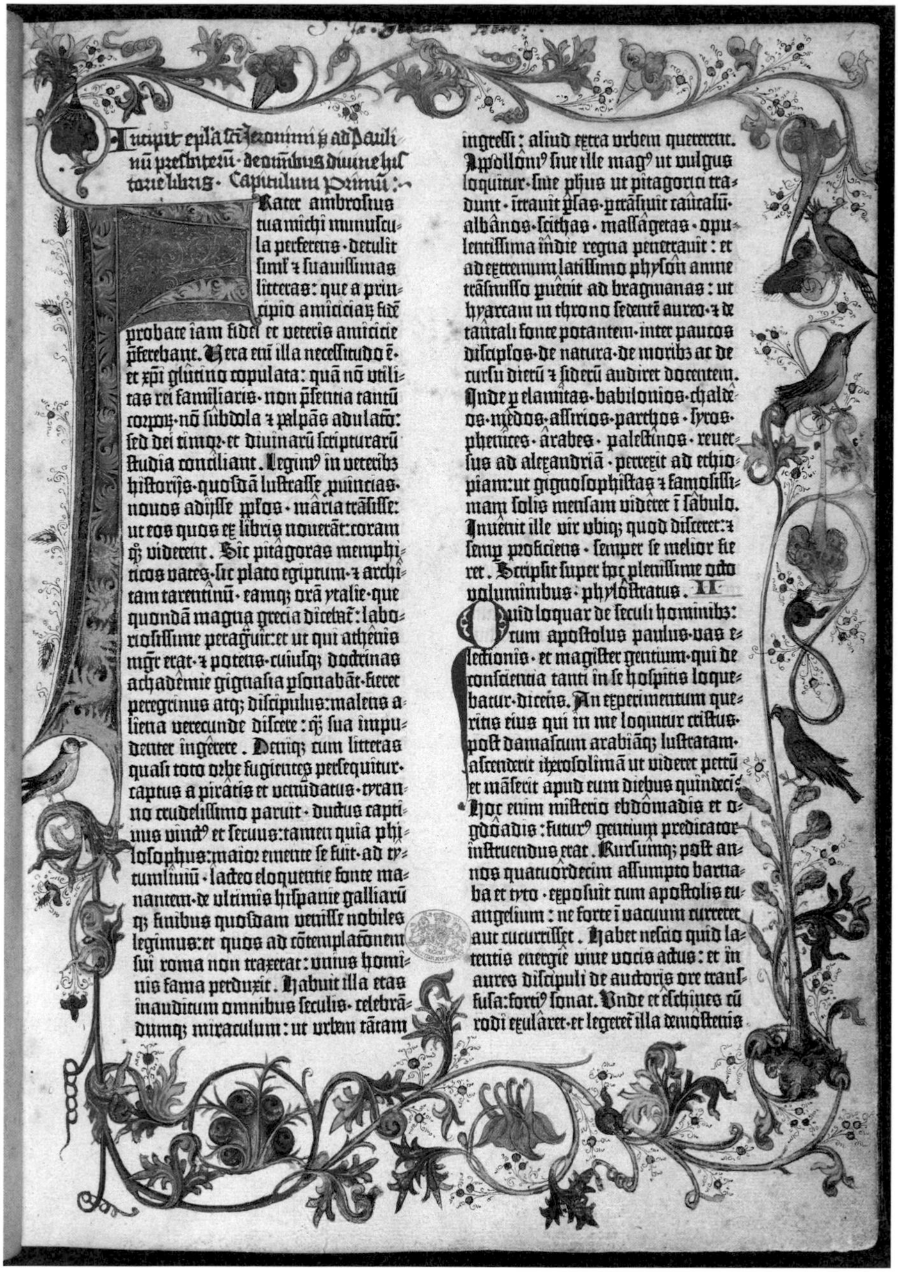

Figure 4.3 Jerome's Epistle to Paulinus, set as the preface to his fourth-century CE Latin translation of the Bible, known as the Vulgate (common) text: the standard translation for western Christianity at the time. From *The (Gutenberg) Bible* (1454). Published by Johannes Gutenberg and Johannes Fust, Mainz. British Library, London, C.9.d.3 p.1. Photo: © The British Library Board

for an **octavo** book (this word comes from the Latin for 'eight', signifying eight leaves of paper in each gathering).

Now you need to cut the page edges. So, keeping the left-hand fold intact to make the spine, trim the other three edges to open up the pages. Then number each page: you should have 16 in total. Now open them out and put them back together as a sheet of A4, remembering to get your hand-drawn marks back together. What do you observe?

Discussion

This is the printer's view of your little book: pages out of sequence, aligned in two different directions on each side of the paper. This layout is the guide for how the eight pages of type destined for one side of the paper would be laid out and locked together before being placed on the bed of the press.

Early modern printers did mark pages to keep track of the many pages they were printing. Take a close look at a typical example of a relatively affordable volume: the very popular and much reprinted text of a collection of one of the first magazines of the early eighteenth century, *The Spectator*. I own one example, spotted in a second-hand bookshop for less than the price of a new paperback novel. Here it is, in Figure 4.4, looking a bit battered. Figure 4.5 shows the detail of the gatherings, revealed because part of the sewing of the binding that would normally hide them has come away as a result of much use. Opening the book at the start of a gathering reveals how the printer uses a printed code letter to show him (or, rarely, her) which pages of text belong together: this is gathering B (Figure 4.6). The printer has also reminded himself that the sheet belongs in volume 3, by printing 'VOL. III' in the lower corner.

The handpress process deconstructs the steady flow of the author's work to such an extent that it is remarkable that it gets put back together in a readable form at the end of the process. Missing words, missing lines, pages from one book printed on the back of pages for another book, gatherings left out of the final piles of folded pages: human error creates the potential for all of these problems.

An unusual, but significant, stage in a book's life cycle can come when it re-enters the market as a rare and valuable object (an afterlife as collector's object). Damaged books of this quality can be remade. Making up a new book from older parts has been a book collector's

Figure 4.4 Open copy, showing binding, of *The Spectator*, volume III (1739). Published by J. and R. Tonson, London. Photo: © Malcolm Daisley

Figure 4.5 The gatherings of *The Spectator*, volume III (1739). Published by J. and R. Tonson, London. Photo: © Malcolm Daisley

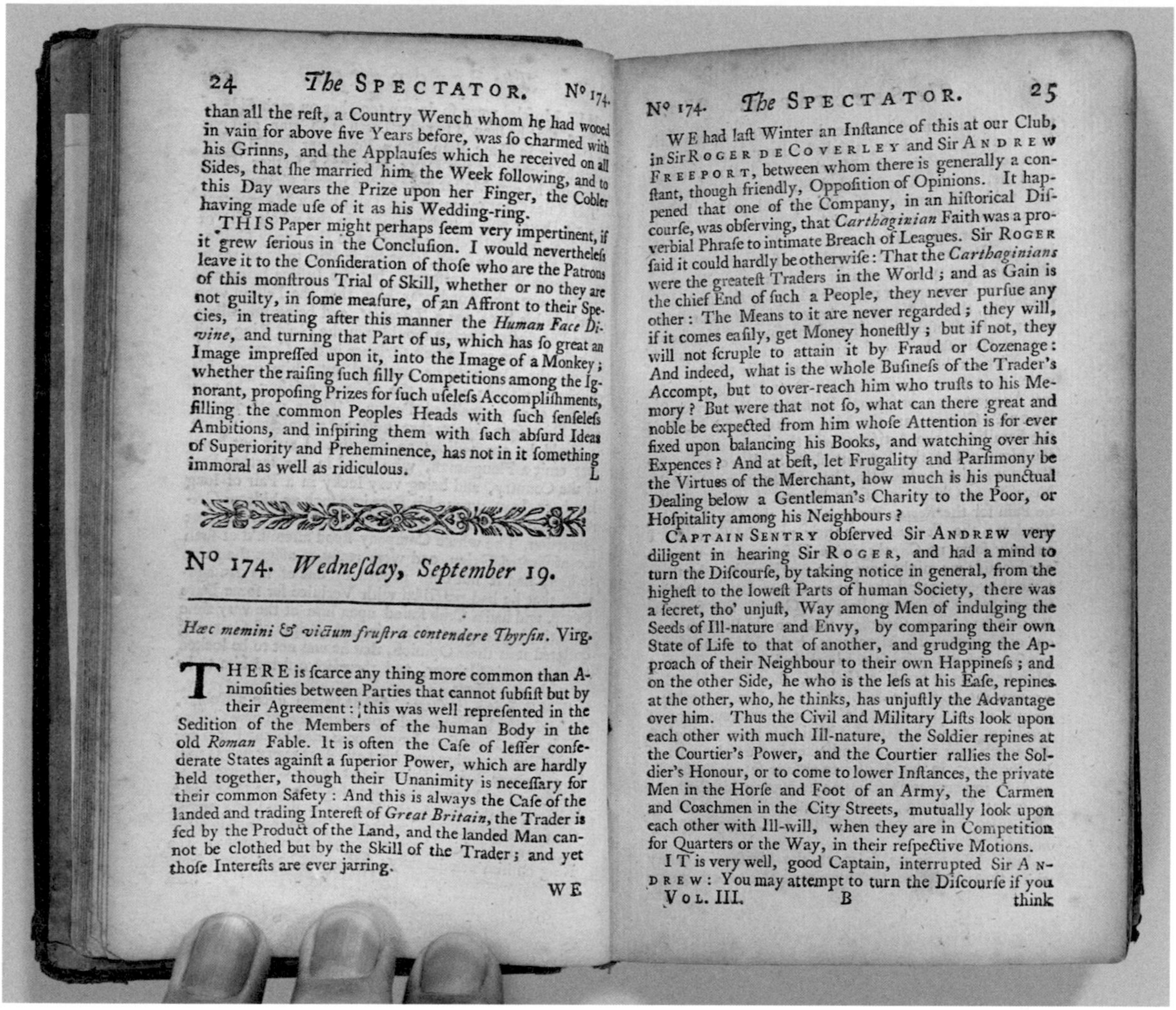

24 *The* SPECTATOR. N° 174.

than all the reſt, a Country Wench whom he had wooed in vain for above five Years before, was ſo charmed with his Grinns, and the Applauſes which he received on all Sides, that ſhe married him the Week following, and to this Day wears the Prize upon her Finger, the Cobler having made uſe of it as his Wedding-ring.

THIS Paper might perhaps ſeem very impertinent, if it grew ſerious in the Concluſion. I would nevertheleſs leave it to the Conſideration of thoſe who are the Patrons of this monſtrous Trial of Skill, whether or no they are not guilty, in ſome meaſure, of an Affront to their Species, in treating after this manner the *Human Face Divine*, and turning that Part of us, which has ſo great an Image impreſſed upon it, into the Image of a Monkey; whether the raiſing ſuch ſilly Competitions among the Ignorant, propoſing Prizes for ſuch uſeleſs Accompliſhments, filling the common Peoples Heads with ſuch ſenſeleſs Ambitions, and inſpiring them with ſuch abſurd Ideas of Superiority and Preheminence, has not in it ſomething immoral as well as ridiculous. L

N° 174. *Wedneſday, September* 19.

Hæc memini & victum fruſtra contendere Thyrſin. Virg.

THERE is ſcarce any thing more common than Animoſities between Parties that cannot ſubſiſt but by their Agreement: this was well repreſented in the Sedition of the Members of the human Body in the old *Roman* Fable. It is often the Caſe of leſſer confederate States againſt a ſuperior Power, which are hardly held together, though their Unanimity is neceſſary for their common Safety: And this is always the Caſe of the landed and trading Intereſt of *Great Britain*, the Trader is fed by the Product of the Land, and the landed Man cannot be clothed but by the Skill of the Trader; and yet thoſe Intereſts are ever jarring.

WE

N° 174. *The* SPECTATOR. 25

WE had laſt Winter an Inſtance of this at our Club, in Sir ROGER DE COVERLEY and Sir ANDREW FREEPORT, between whom there is generally a conſtant, though friendly, Oppoſition of Opinions. It happened that one of the Company, in an hiſtorical Diſcourſe, was obſerving, that *Carthaginian* Faith was a proverbial Phraſe to intimate Breach of Leagues. Sir ROGER ſaid it could hardly be otherwiſe: That the *Carthaginians* were the greateſt Traders in the World; and as Gain is the chief End of ſuch a People, they never purſue any other: The Means to it are never regarded; they will, if it comes eaſily, get Money honeſtly; but if not, they will not ſcruple to attain it by Fraud or Cozenage: And indeed, what is the whole Buſineſs of the Trader's Accompt, but to over-reach him who truſts to his Memory? But were that not ſo, what can there great and noble be expected from him whoſe Attention is for ever fixed upon balancing his Books, and watching over his Expences? And at beſt, let Frugality and Parſimony be the Virtues of the Merchant, how much is his punctual Dealing below a Gentleman's Charity to the Poor, or Hoſpitality among his Neighbours?

CAPTAIN SENTRY obſerved Sir ANDREW very diligent in hearing Sir ROGER, and had a mind to turn the Diſcourſe, by taking notice in general, from the higheſt to the loweſt Parts of human Society, there was a ſecret, tho' unjuſt, Way among Men of indulging the Seeds of Ill-nature and Envy, by comparing their own State of Life to that of another, and grudging the Approach of their Neighbour to their own Happineſs; and on the other Side, he who is the leſs at his Eaſe, repines at the other, who, he thinks, has unjuſtly the Advantage over him. Thus the Civil and Military Liſts look upon each other with much Ill-nature, the Soldier repines at the Courtier's Power, and the Courtier rallies the Soldier's Honour, or to come to lower Inſtances, the private Men in the Horſe and Foot of an Army, the Carmen and Coachmen in the City Streets, mutually look upon each other with Ill-will, when they are in Competition for Quarters or the Way, in their reſpective Motions.

IT is very well, good Captain, interrupted Sir ANDREW: You may attempt to turn the Diſcourſe if you

VOL. III. B think

Figure 4.6 Pages 24 and 25 of *The Spectator*, volume III (1739). Published by J. and R. Tonson, London. Photo: © Malcolm Daisley. The bottom of the right-hand page shows the printer's code and volume marks (in this case, B and Vol. III)

solution to the problem of an imperfect copy of a nonetheless collectable book; in effect, the remade book has an art market value in much the same way that an over-restored antique has. The printer's metadata can be used as evidence for whether a book has been taken apart and reassembled from fragments of other copies before being rebound.

The other area where departures may have been made from the author's work concerns the **compositor**, or the person assembling the type. Early modern compositors combined the roles of copy-editor, graphic designer and typesetter: they were judge and jury on the spelling, grammar and layout of the text. Their interventions could result in major errors in the printing house, which readers often needed to be aware of in order to assess the quality of the end product, in ways which we no longer have to consider. These historic contexts that create variations between copies of the same work need to be understood by professional rare book librarians, who catalogue individual books. The catalogues need to reflect the range of variation possible, so rare book specialists need the skills of close looking and comparison in order to create object descriptions. This is why this chapter treats the early modern book as an object which is solid, but unstable.

4.2 The early book trade

The early modern trade in books was organised around booksellers, as the link between authors, the associated print trades and readers. Booksellers would be described as 'publishers' in today's book trade terminology. Gutenberg and the early adopters of print technology up until around 1600 tended to combine all the functions of printing, distributing and retail sales. After 1600, these functions increasingly separated out, particularly in major centres of printing such as capital cities.

Figure 4.7 shows the publisher's credit in my volume of *The Spectator*, which states 'LONDON: Printed for J. and R. TONSON, at *Shakespear's-Head*, over-against *Catharine-street* in the *Strand*. MDCCXXXIX.' The booksellers (publishers) were J. and R. Tonson, whose address, in the absence of a street numbering system, was at the sign of Shakespeare's Head, in London. The Tonsons would have described themselves as booksellers (publishing from an office, distributing from a warehouse and making retail sales from a shop), since 'publisher' is a term adopted in the book trade only after about 1800 (Feather, 2007).

The first English bookseller was William Caxton (1415~24–1492), a merchant who established a successful career in Europe and then decided to move into the new world of printing. Caxton was the first bookseller to print a book in the English language, *A History of Troy*, which he translated himself from French in 1474. It was printed in his own printing workshop in Bruges (in modern-day Belgium), with copies exported to England. By late 1476 Caxton had returned to England, bringing with him the first press to be set up there, on which he printed *The Canterbury Tales* by Geoffrey Chaucer (*c*.1340–1400).

Thus, almost 21 years after Gutenberg had printed his great Bible, the emergent print industry reached England. One of the consequences of this, as explored in the next section, is that more versions of favourite or authoritative texts were produced and circulated. This meant that publishers and readers became more aware of differences in how an author's works were treated. Understanding which, if any, version was most faithful to an original (if an early manuscript existed) became a new challenge for early modern scholars.

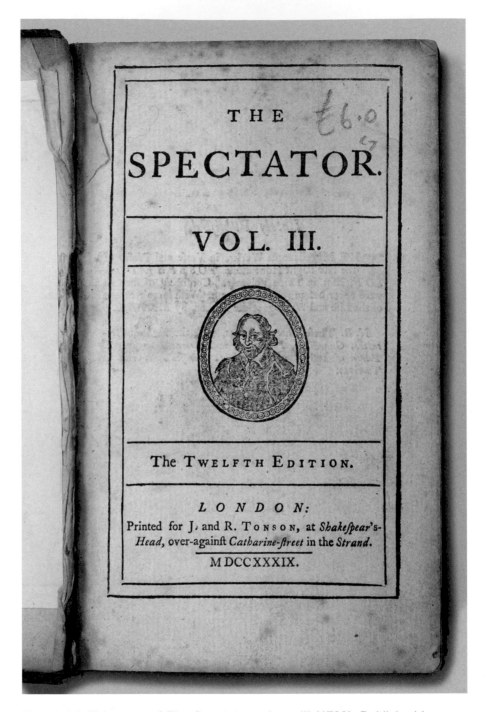

Figure 4.7 Title page of *The Spectator*, volume III (1739). Published by
J. and R. Tonson, London. Photo: © Malcolm Daisley

The rise of critical practice

The examples of Caxton's production of the first printed book in English (his translation of a French text) and his subsequent version of a book previously available only in manuscript copies (Chaucer's *Canterbury Tales*) provide a powerful reminder that books are not simply copies of a unique original. Both of Caxton's early books required a process of selection and editing – even a change of language in the case of the *History of Troy*. The *Canterbury Tales* were particularly problematic to work from, since Chaucer did not finish the work before he died and the first manuscript copies (not supervised by the author) are variations on presenting a readable sequence of the tales. Indeed, after Caxton's death his business was carried on in London by his associate Wynken de Worde (d.1535), who continued to produce new versions of the *Tales*. Which version should readers choose to read?

The very existence of printed versions of older texts, previously only accessible in limited manuscript copies, posed new challenges for readers. The book historian Lotte Hellinga makes the point that the availability of printed books changed scholarly practice. The circulation of the new printed versions encouraged scholar readers to compare texts in order to see what had been added, changed or otherwise edited. This new critical approach to differences between texts remains at the heart of modern scholarly work. The following activity invites you to consider the historical circumstances of Chaucer's literary work and the subsequent treatment of it by early printers.

Activity

Read the two passages below. The first extract summarises the circumstances of Chaucer's creation of *The Canterbury Tales*, left unfinished at his death in 1400. In the second extract, Hellinga reflects on the rapid change in intellectual understanding of how to verify the content of a text and its relationship to an earlier (perhaps lost) work by the author. This extract mentions de Worde, the bookseller who worked for Caxton and took over on his death.

What did de Worde do in order to produce his new edition of Chaucer?

In your answer, reflect on your understanding that text and object can come together in a series of variations, as a result of material changes introduced by the production process. Author, translator, editor, typesetter and printer may all be involved here.

You should allow about 40 minutes for this activity.

How do you think this new critical practice towards texts might be similar to what you understand about ideas for classifying and describing objects?

Extract 1

[*The Canterbury Tales*] was left unfinished: the extant version consists of about 17,000 lines of verse and prose, in ten fragments. Just over eighty manuscripts survive, of which fifty-five are complete or nearly complete. The earliest, from the early fifteenth century, is the Hengwrt manuscript (in the National Library of Wales), which has a text apparently close to what Chaucer wrote, but a rather disjointed ordering of the tales; the slightly later Ellesmere manuscript (in the Huntington Library, San Marino, California), carefully written and produced and containing excellent miniatures, has most frequently been used as the base text for modern editions. In fact, what most readers think of as *The Canterbury Tales* is the Ellesmere version, an attempt (sometimes a distinctly editorial one) to present the fragments that Chaucer left in a coherent form, but not what Chaucer himself would have eventually published.

(Gray, 2004 [2012])

Extract 2

De Worde's revision of *The Canterbury Tales*, based on the comparison of several manuscript sources [...], is a good example of a remarkable phenomenon that began to develop as an effect of the much-expanded availability of textual sources, which is in direct contradiction to what must have appeared initially to be the major advantage of the multiplication of texts in print. A printed version might indeed be accepted as a standard and be copied in subsequent editions without being subjected to further critical assessment. However, multiplying a text in many copies might initiate a critical process. It frequently happened that on publication in print a text was compared with other sources and improved in later editions, sometimes on the grounds of greater completeness, but also by the introduction of variant readings, by conjecture, through **collation** [comparison] with manuscripts, or in due course with other printed editions with versions from independent sources. The process can be observed from the very first years of printing, and can be demonstrated particularly well in the successive editions of *The Canterbury Tales*. It accelerated to become in the sixteenth century the basis for the critical assessment of the complete European literary heritage from classical times onward. Its immediate impact on religion and society was never felt more dramatically than in the sixteenth century, but in essence the process continues to the present day.

(Hellinga, 2007)

Discussion

Chaucer died in 1400, but the first extract suggests that the earliest manuscript version of the *Tales* was created after his death, during the early 1400s. The second extract shows that de Worde decided to produce his own edition of Chaucer, by going back to some of the available manuscript copies and making his own decisions about how to edit this complex text. Hellinga lists the ways in which a printed text could relate to an earlier form of the work, which suggests that in the case of problematic fragments or multiple versions of texts there is no single 'work' to provide the definitive standard for reproductions. Thinking of these in terms of object analysis and classification, these multiple texts can be collected and treated as an assemblage, to be analysed for their similarities and differences, perhaps even helping to find a chronological order where the dates of creation are uncertain.

The origins of critical practice are important not just for literature but for all the humanities subjects, and this is the foundation of teaching the humanities as well as researching them. The impetus that print reproduction gave to scholarship raised issues of how to trust something in print; issues that were more problematic than they had been in the practice of copying medieval manuscripts. The rise of critical practice had particular effects during the seventeenth century, when scholars used the comparative method to question inherited scientific knowledge and turned to make their own observations from the material world. Today we remain concerned about how to verify documents in very different media. This is a critical problem, not simply for scholars wanting to understand Chaucer, but as an issue of citizenship, too. (The ability to assess sources critically and to trace their origins is crucial not just for journalists and policymakers today, but also for ordinary readers (and voters) who want to make informed judgements.) In many ways, the current 'open' nature of the web, allowing self-publishing, plagiarism and the creative reuse of materials – as well as varying standards of design and user-friendliness – parallels the early state of the print industry. The phrase 'trusted content' is often used now to describe web-based information that stands up to critical scrutiny.

The book as an object can be examined not just in terms of technology and the evolution of the production process (the history of science and technology), but also in relation to how the particular qualities of this object were used and had their own impact on the users. This is the social life of the object, the evidence for its cultural history. Books can be defined less in terms of their overt function (as carrying text that people read from) and more in terms of how people use them as tools to enable them to do other things in their lives: sometimes in their outward social roles and sometimes in their interior personal thoughts. Books that are treated as tools also take on different meanings, according to the uses they are put to and to the variety of their users: the social contexts. To find the evidence for the cultural work that books can do requires some closer investigation of what goes into a book.

4.3 Beyond text: the frontispiece

The first image in a book, ahead of the main text (which may have its own illustrations), is called a **frontispiece**, often visible as a decorative way of presenting the title of the work. It was not a feature of medieval manuscripts but seems to have become common in printed books during the seventeenth century (Barchas, 2003, p. 21). A portrait of the author may also be used as a frontispiece. All these images were made from a different technology from that of movable metal type. The technology of the handpress era for reproducing images was the **copper plate**, literally a sheet of copper, on which finely engraved lines on the metal surface were reproduced as inked lines on paper. The discussion here concentrates on frontispiece author portraits, as a powerful example of how the material form of the book had expanded by the seventeenth century to include the virtual presence of the author, in the form of their image.

Early portrait frontispieces tended to follow the art conventions of how portraits were styled. The artist might include objects to suggest the sitter's occupation: weapons to denote a soldier, for instance, or a laurel wreath for a political leader, or books as a reminder of an author's other works. These parts of the image that can be treated as symbols, as conveying meanings, are iconographic. The reader could enter into the illusion that the author deserved the status of having a portrait or a bust created, and that the tributes heaped around them represented the cultural values the author deserved to have attributed to them. Readers during the seventeenth and eighteenth centuries would have been familiar with these conventions and the iconography they entailed, as they were also used in looseleaf images of personalities that could be bought in bookshops and collected. Today frontispieces take on a life beyond the book when old books are dismantled in order that the images they contain may be saved as collectable prints.

Images of Shakespeare: a true likeness?

William Shakespeare (1564–1616), a national icon in the UK today, was also the most influential English playwright by the end of his career. It was not standard practice to publish the texts of contemporary plays. It was a significant innovation for his friend and fellow playwright Ben Jonson (1572–1637) to organise the formal publication of Shakespeare's

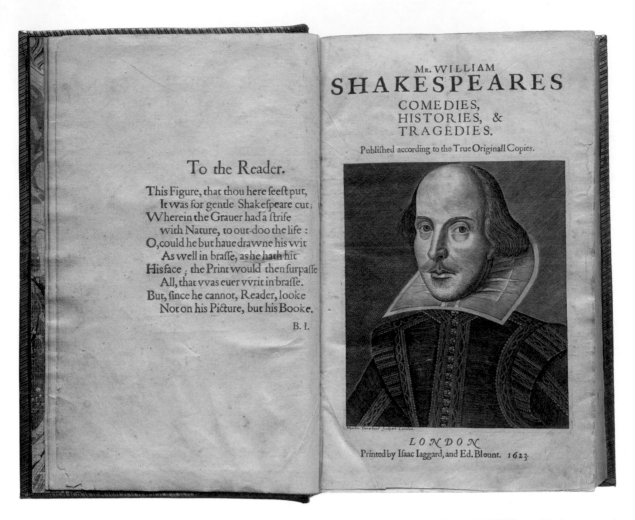

To the Reader.

This Figure, that thou here feeft put,
    It was for gentle Shakefpeare cut;
Wherein the Grauer had a ftrife
    with Nature, to out-doo the life :
O, could he but haue drawne his wit
    As well in braffe, as he hath hit
Hisface ; the Print would then furpaffe
    All, that vvas euer vvrit in braffe.
But, fince he cannot, Reader, looke
    Not on his Picture, but his Booke.

                                    B. I.

Mr. WILLIAM
SHAKESPEARES
COMEDIES,
HISTORIES, &
TRAGEDIES.

Publifhed according to the True Originall Copies.

LONDON
Printed by Ifaac Iaggard, and Ed. Blount. 1623.

Figure 4.8 Martin Droeshout, Portrait of William Shakespeare, engraving from *Mr William Shakespeare's Comedies, Histories and Tragedies: Published According to the True Original Copies* (1623). Published by Isaac Jaggard and Ed. Blount, London. Folger Shakespeare Library, Washington, DC, STC 22273 fo.1 no.5. By permission of the Folger Shakespeare Library

collected prose and plays (but not his poems) seven years after his death, in 1623.

The resulting publication was the first time a playwright in the English language had their output printed. Jonson chose an expensive format, the folio – something that might be thought of as a collector's format. The large page size meant that this book was not intended to be carried around and used for actors' performances, but to be kept for private reading, by people who could afford the high price. Just 220 copies of this publication – the First Folio – are known to survive, from an original print run of perhaps only 750 (Blayney, 1991).

The First Folio author portrait is positioned on the title page, an example of the great range of variation visible in the layout of books at this time (see Figure 4.8). The portrait consists only of the head and shoulders of a man in Elizabethan clothes and the text 'Martin Droeshout Sculpsit London' in the bottom left – 'sculpsit' being the Latin word used to indicate that Droeshout was the engraver. The reader is asked to take it that this is a true likeness of Shakespeare.

Another version of a portrait of Shakespeare has already appeared in this chapter, on the title page of the volume of *The Spectator* discussed earlier (see Figure 4.7). The booksellers J. and R. Tonson inherited their business from their father and great-uncle, who were both keen to promote Shakespeare as a leading English author and who printed a (then) new revised edition of his works. While they also championed other English authors, the fact that the Tonsons used Shakespeare's image as their 'brand identity' signalled a particular sense of ownership (and the firm literally owned the copyrights to Shakespeare's works). As Shakespeare's literary reputation increased over time, all artefacts about his life and time have been closely scrutinised. One major art exhibition in 2006, for instance, put a range of visual and material culture associated with him on display. Shakespeare's face has become 'a visual emblem of English literary achievement' (Cooper, 2006, p. 9).

It has become very important to know what Shakespeare looked like, and there are now three versions of his face that are generally accepted as authentic: the Droeshout engraving, the sculpted bust on Shakespeare's memorial in the church in Stratford-upon-Avon, and an oil painting known as the 'Cobbe Shakespeare' (because it has been in the possession of the Cobbe family for at least 300 years). The latter is the basis for other oil paintings of the playwright and for the image that Droeshout worked from. The search for a true likeness of Shakespeare has been a highly contested matter – but, if they had not seen him in person, the early modern readers of Shakespeare's collected works would have had to take it on trust that he was accurately represented on the title page.

Activity

You should now complete the online activity 'John Donne and the frontispiece', which you can find on the Study Planner of the module website. This activity allows you to explore the frontispiece to another seventeenth-century text: John Donne's *Devotions*, first published in 1638.

You should allow about an hour for this activity.

4.4 Cover stories: historic bindings

Buying a book marked the stage at which the early modern book left the bookseller's domain and entered the social world of the owner. The rest of this chapter discusses the many ways in which post-production uses of the book can leave their mark (the consumption stage of the object life cycle). The binding of the book is the most obvious feature here. Early modern books could be sold in plain temporary paper or card covers, for the purchaser to replace with their choice of leather binding. Some title pages at this time display different prices for the book depending on whether it was 'stitched' (with the gatherings sewn together, but having no cover) or 'bound' (having a finished cover), suggesting that the bookseller offered both forms for sale (Pearson, 2005, p. 8). The cover of a book – its outer binding – was not, however, part of the design and marketing of the object then, as it is now.

David Pearson describes how 'all bindings from the hand-press era are essentially unique objects' and can be treated as artworks, because of the materials, construction and decoration techniques involved in creating them (see the box on 'Covers and bindings'), reflecting the binders' workshops where they were made (Pearson, 2005, p. x). Pearson's decades of experience of handling and researching historic bindings informs this edited selection of his findings (Pearson, 2005, pp. x–xi):

- If you locate twenty copies of the same sixteenth-, seventeenth- or eighteenth-century book which survive in their contemporary bindings, those bindings will almost certainly display considerable variety.

- Books were often not bound where they were printed, and the place of printing is not necessarily a guide to the place where they were bound.

- The date of printing is, likewise, no sure guide to the date of binding. Books have, over the centuries, regularly been re-bound for various reasons.

- The fashion of the day was always changing, following wider trends in design and ornament.

These points suggest that the evidence for the date, place and workshop where the binding originated (and possibly the patron who commissioned it) is held within the binding itself, rather than within the text it enfolds. Pearson's findings also carry a warning about books that have been rebound. 'The great classics of Elizabethan and Jacobean literature, along with many other books which became collectable long after they were printed, are often found today in heavily gilt goatskin bindings put on in the nineteenth century, a reflection of the values of that period' (Pearson, 2005, p. 2). As historic books became artefacts in a market valuing them for their historic status (namely, the antiquarian book trade), collectors in the past frequently upgraded a modest binding to match the cultural value they attributed to the text. The binding thus became treated as an artistic frame for the text, rather than as a historic artefact worthy of preservation in its own right. This runs counter to modern conservation practice, which is to repair and reattach damaged historic bindings. A historic book should not be judged by its cover.

Covers and bindings

Leather was the dominant book covering during the handpress era, and calfskin was the dominant type of leather – usually dyed brown. Some books had cheaper parchment covers, pale cream in colour – and you might spot these distinctive undecorated bindings in a historic library. Leather is soft enough to bear the impression of metal tools, so binding designs are created by the contrasts between the negative impressions (dints) left by tools and the smooth untooled surface. The negative impressions can be filled in with gold leaf, to pick out the design, in which case the results are described as 'gold-tooled' (see Figure 4.9). This technique originated in the Arab world in the thirteenth century and reached Europe through Italian trading ports such as Venice (Pearson, 2005, p. 50).

If the tooling is ungilded (not filled in with gold leaf), it is described as 'blind-tooled' (see Figure 4.10). Larger motifs covering much of the surface area are called 'panel stamps'. Panels could be realistic, figurative scenes (for example, depicting scenes from the Bible); or naturalistic (showing roses or foliage, for instance); or heraldic, including displays of the royal arms (although this was not necessarily indicative of royal ownership). By 1600, panel stamps were created to put a complete design on to a cover for smaller books, and abstract, linear designs called arabesques (a sixteenth-century European name derived from the designs' origins in Islamic art) became dominant. Later designs could be highly elaborate, using styles found in fashionable interiors and motifs created to complement the text (see Figure 4.11).

Simpler bindings were ornamented just with ruled lines, creating a frame, sometimes set off by a small motif in the centre.

My *Spectator* volume has been bound using a standard design of ruled lines, typical of its early eighteenth-century date. The front and back covers just have a pair of parallel lines inscribed around the edges and then gilded. The spine shows the bumps in the leather where bands of stitching keep the gatherings together. There are six equal divisions on the spine, which are picked out with more pairs of gilded lines (see Figure 4.4).

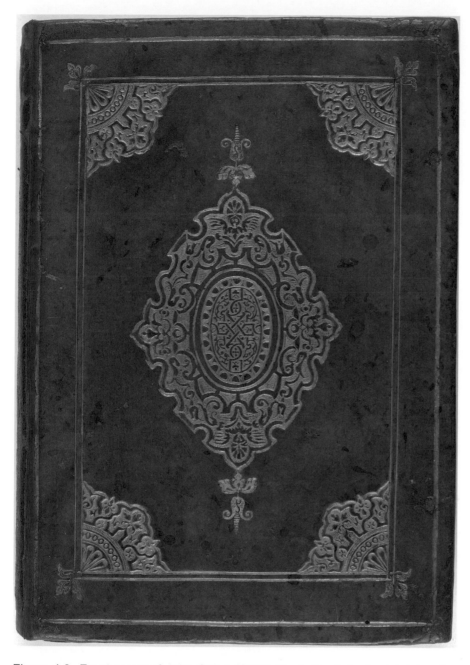

Figure 4.9 Front cover of John Caius (1574) *De Antiquitate Cantabrigiensis Academiae Libri Duo*. Published by J. Daij, London. British Library, London, Davis 61. Photo: © The British Library Board. Quarto, gold-tooled brown calf, bound at Matthew Parker's Lambeth Palace bindery

Figure 4.10 Typical book binding of the period 1500–1800, from Caspar Shatzger (1527) *Scrutinium Divinae Scripturae*. Published in Tübingen. British Library, London, Davis 16. Photo: © The British Library Board. Octavo, blind-tooled brown calf using panel stamps

Figure 4.11 Front cover of Marmaduke Stalkartt (1781) *Naval Architecture*.
Published for the author, London. British Library, London, 62.g.8. Photo:
© The British Library Board

Activity

You should allow about 45 minutes for this activity.

You should now watch the film 'Anatomy of a book', which you can find on the module website. In this film, different copies of a historic work on anatomy are discussed and compared. The book is by the Dutch anatomist Frederik Ruysch (1638–1731). It is called *Opera Omnia Anatomico-medico-chirurgica* ('Collected works of anatomy, medicine and surgery') and was published in Amsterdam.

The film examines the material features of this eighteenth-century book. As you jot down notes about the film, pay attention to the physical characteristics of the different copies introduced here.

How does the case of Ruysch's *Opera Omnia* illustrate the value of investigating the physical evidence of handpress-era books?

Discussion

The film identifies why three copies of a book, all ascribed to the same author and given the same title, are not the same book. The bindings concerned are all in different styles: two dating from the eighteenth century and one from the late nineteenth century. The one with the most recent binding has untrimmed pages, reflecting the state in which the book left the printer's workshop. (Trimmed pages not only look neat, they also flatten out the paper and keep dust out.) One of the copies has a **bookplate** bearing a date that is earlier than the date when the book was printed, so it was probably pasted in by mistake when the Cambridge University Library finally sorted out the books given to it by George I (1660–1727; reigned 1714–27). This is a good example of a misleading piece of evidence (the bookplate was created for an event that had nothing to do with the book it was eventually pasted into).

The film also explains that all three copies are made up of several different and separate items, available either individually (like a magazine) or bound up together. This was a clever bit of marketing by the printer – taking advantage of the author's reputation, he reprinted the cheaper, smaller book published in 1687 in a more expensive, larger format (the **quarto** size). This explains why the copies do not have continuous page numbers, but are divided by new title pages and frontispieces, some with different dates from that on the first title page.

Overall, looking at the size, number of illustrations and standard of production, this quarto format represented a big investment by the printer. This leaves us with the question of who might have wanted to buy all the different parts and have them bound up – it must have been someone wealthy with a serious interest in the knowledge that the work represented.

Collections of books

The seventeenth-century diarist and naval official Samuel Pepys (1633–1703) wrote about his interest in how his books were bound. His library survives to this day, allowing us to make comparisons between what Pepys said he liked and what he actually owned. In practice, Pepys seems to have gone along with the binding fashions of his time: 'his desire as a customer to influence the actual design choices seems to have been less than we might at first expect' (Pearson, 2005, p. 11). Pepys wanted his collection of 3000 volumes to survive for posterity, so he bequeathed it to a college (Magdalene) at Cambridge University, along with his 12 purpose-made bookcases, where it remains today. As a result, his library makes a good case study in terms of the bindings purchased and commissioned by a keen reader at the end of the seventeenth century (Nixon, 1984).

Pepys is today most famous for his diaries, where he recorded some of his interest in books. For instance, he wrote on 8 July 1664: 'So to Pauls churchyard about my books – and to the binders and directed the doing of my Chaucer, though they were not full near enough for me, but pretty well it is – and thence to the clasp-makers to have it clasped and bossed' (quoted in Nixon, 1984, p. xiii). The binding of this Chaucer volume is shown in Figure 4.12, with the brass clasps and studs ('bosses') that Pepys mentions – these provide extra protection to the leather binding. Many of the books in Pepys' library use this style of binding, with or without the brass additions. Another favourite style is more elaborate (see Figure 4.13), created by using triangular tools on the leather 'with a design suggesting ironwork' (Nixon, 1984, p. xvii). Pepys received gifts of beautifully bound books from people keen to win his approval, either in his official capacity as a government official in the Admiralty or, as in the case of Figure 4.14, from a musician who had been employed in his household, Cesare Morelli.

Figure 4.12 Typical book binding from Samuel Pepys' library: from Geoffrey Chaucer (1602) *Works*. Published by Adam Islip, London. Magdalene College, Cambridge, 2365. Photo: The Pepys Library, Magdalene College, Cambridge

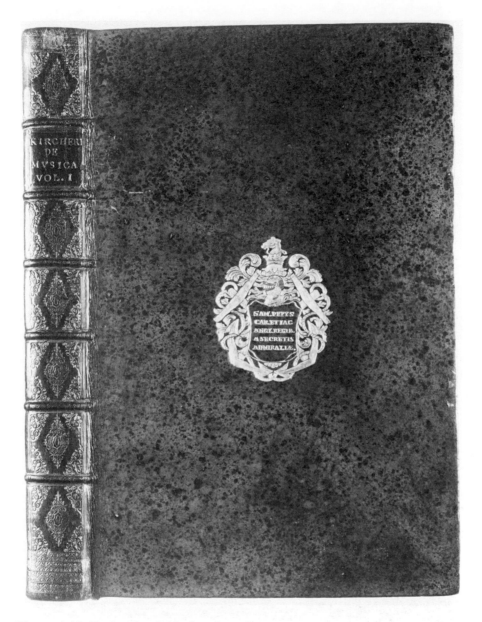

Figure 4.13 Typical book binding from Samuel Pepys' library: from
Athanasius Kircher (1650) *Musurgia Universalis*, volume I. Published by
Franciscus Corbellet, Rome. Magdalene College, Cambridge, 2467. Photo:
The Pepys Library, Magdalene College, Cambridge

Figure 4.14 Typical book binding from Samuel Pepys' library: from the collection of music manuscripts bound and labelled *Musick* (1693). Magdalene College, Cambridge, 2591. Photo: The Pepys Library, Magdalene College, Cambridge

Activity

Reading 4.1 is an extract from an article by the book historian Rowan Watson, 'Some non-textual uses of books' (2007). This article was originally published in *A Companion to the History of the Book*, edited by Simon Eliot and Jonathan Rose. The discussion considers manuscript and printed books, and some of the uses of the codex that are as historic as the format of the book.

Read through the extract now. Why do you think that the codex has so many uses?

You should allow about an hour for this activity.

Discussion

My answer to this concerns how portable a codex is: when stitched together and covered, it is a nice solid object. As small units, such volumes can easily be reproduced and stored for retrieval, on shelves which are good for displaying books (to reinforce the points about status made in the reading). Many of the examples of social practices around books provided in the extract concern the need to see or to touch a book, or indeed to be seen with a book. Prayer-books as fashion accessories – a worldly use at odds with the purpose of the books' content – provide one example of an object being used against the grain, as it were; the extract notes that this was a fourteenth-century criticism of wealthy Parisian housewives.

4.5 Owners' and readers' marks

Beyond the binding, owners and readers can make other additions to their books. These can be divided into 'marks of ownership' and 'marks about reading'. As with bindings, individual examples of these marks can be admired for their artistic qualities or for their historic significance, but collectively they can be assembled into a picture of owners' and readers' interactions with the book as an object, as well as representing their intellectual engagement with the text.

Marks of ownership can be printed or written, and can be formal or informal. The simplest practice (still used today) involves writing the owner's name on the **half-title** or title page. Purchasers in the early modern era also did this, occasionally at the same time recording the price they had paid for the book. At the back of my *Spectator* volume, on the blank end-leaf, someone has written 'Cathrine King at Brandon Whites Hart', which is presumably the name of one of the owners – from the Suffolk town called Brandon, perhaps? (See Figure 4.15.)

Formal claims to ownership come in the form of printed bookplates glued on to the inside of the front cover (the paste-down page). Bookplates (rectangular pieces of paper bearing a printed design and, usually, the owner's name) have a long history as a minor branch of the arts associated with books, and can be collector's items in their own right. At some point, my *Spectator* volume left Cathrine King's ownership and became the property of Edward Sisterson, whose bookplate bearing the date 1901 covers the paste-down at the front of the book (see Figure 4.16). This design uses the coat of arms granted to the Sisterson family, and their Latin motto *Sis terror sontibus* (since Edward Sisterson was a judge, this is a pun around his name and profession, roughly translating as 'You may be the terror of the guilty').

Bookplates assert the presence of the owner of the book to any other reader (who might remember to return it to where it belongs). Bookplates are interesting examples of paratext that define some of the conditions of the volume's existence in the social world, rather than adding to the description of the main text. They suggest a level of extra care, and expense, on the part of the owner of the physical volume.

Marks of reading are found on the pages of the main text, usually in the margins in the form of handwritten notes. Readers may mark out points of particular interest or significance in the text by using symbols, the most common of which is a 'pointing hand', called by book

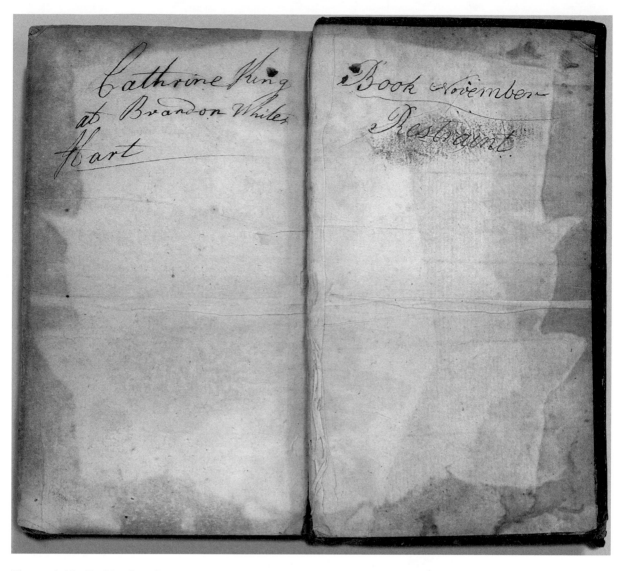

Figure 4.15 End-leaf and paste-down inscriptions from *The Spectator*, volume III (1739). Published by J. and R. Tonson, London. Photo: © Malcolm Daisley

historians a **manicule**. This symbol takes its place in a historic system of learning which has helped students to identify and therefore memorise key points, or 'cleverly contrived or well adapted arguments, brilliant flashes of style, adages, examples, and pithy remarks', as the scholar Erasmus (1466–1536) suggested (quoted in Sherman, 2008, p. 35). Most modern readers do not write in books (even their own), but 'Renaissance readers were not only allowed to write notes in and on their books, they were taught to do so in school' (Sherman, 2008, p. 3).

☞ The 'pointing hand' is also available as a computer icon.

Figure 4.16 Edward Sisterson's bookplate from *The Spectator*, volume III (1739). Published by J. and R. Tonson, London. Photo: © Malcolm Daisley

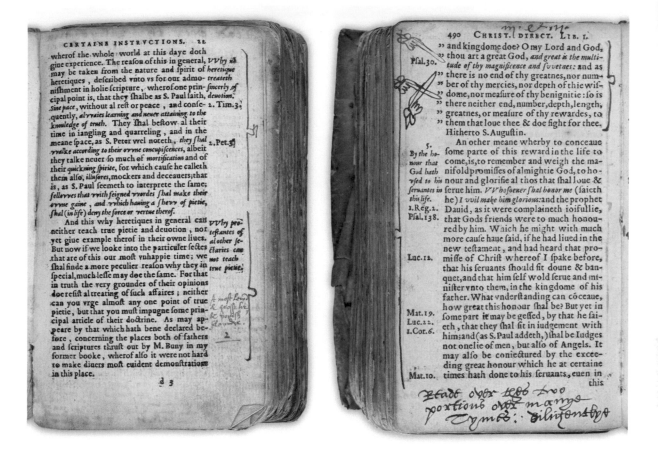

Figure 4.17 Annotations on leaf 22, recto, and on p. 490 of Robert Parsons (1585) *First Booke of the Christian Exercise/A Christian Directorie*. Published by Father Parsons's Press, Rouen. The Huntington Rare Book Department, San Marino, California, RB 433864

Loosely drawn manicules are visible in Figure 4.17, and a very neat version is presented in Figure 4.18.

Early modern readers could also use their notes to express critical opinions. Figure 4.17 shows two examples of different readers' responses to a (Catholic) Christian text, printed in France at a time when England's state religion had become Protestant Christianity and Catholic religious practices and beliefs were outlawed. One reader disagrees vehemently with the author, denouncing a reference to the pope as head of the Roman Catholic Church as 'A most lewd & grosse lie, & popish slander'. Another reader, however, endorses the content, marking what is particularly of interest and commenting: 'Reade over thes two portions over [*sic*] manye Tymes: diligentlye' (Sherman, 2008, p. 10). For historians, such readers' marks are snapshots of diverse

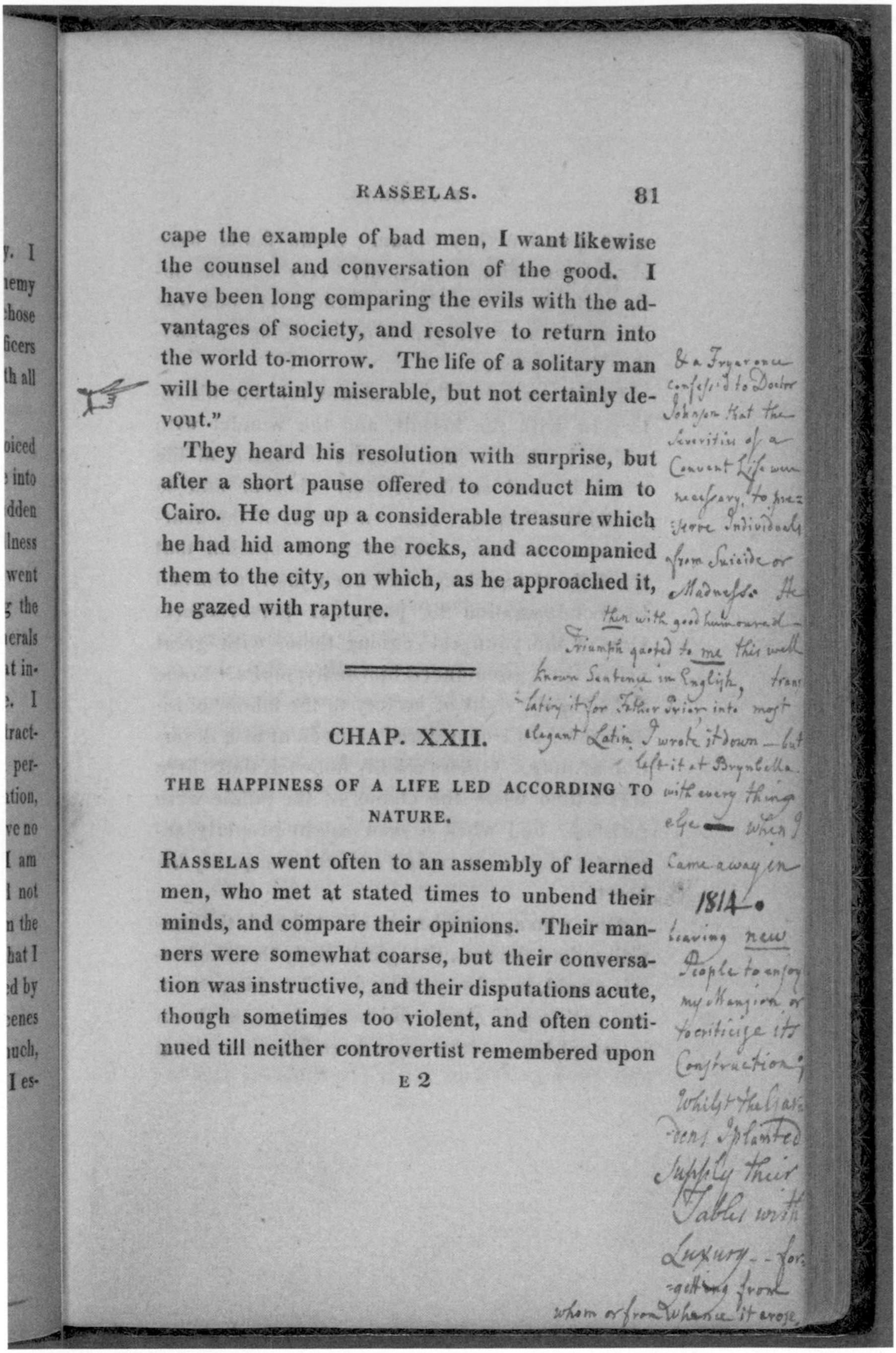

RASSELAS. 81

cape the example of bad men, I want likewise the counsel and conversation of the good. I have been long comparing the evils with the advantages of society, and resolve to return into the world to-morrow. The life of a solitary man will be certainly miserable, but not certainly devout."

They heard his resolution with surprise, but after a short pause offered to conduct him to Cairo. He dug up a considerable treasure which he had hid among the rocks, and accompanied them to the city, on which, as he approached it, he gazed with rapture.

CHAP. XXII.

THE HAPPINESS OF A LIFE LED ACCORDING TO NATURE.

RASSELAS went often to an assembly of learned men, who met at stated times to unbend their minds, and compare their opinions. Their manners were somewhat coarse, but their conversation was instructive, and their disputations acute, though sometimes too violent, and often continued till neither controvertist remembered upon

E 2

& a Fryar once confess'd to Doctor Johnson that the severities of a Convent Life were necessary, to preserve Individuals from Suicide or Madness. He then with good humoured Triumph quoted to me this well known Sentence in English, translating it for Father Prior into most elegant Latin. I wrote it down — but left it at Brynbella with every thing else — when I came away in 1814. leaving new People to enjoy my Mansion or to criticize its Construction; Whilst the Gardens I planted Supply their Tables with Luxury — forgetting from whom or from whence it arose.

Figure 4.18 Example of a pointing hand, in Samuel Johnson (1818) *Rasselas*. Published by John Sharpe, London. Houghton Library, Harvard University, EC75.P6598.Zz818j. The notes and drawing of the hand were provided by the book's original owner, Hester Piozzi responses to the arguments and issues of their time. They are material evidence of intellectual activities and also of the physical process behind reading the book as an object, bringing to the fore the readers who depart from the smooth process of reading in order to create their own paratexts.

We do not know which reader made their comments first, but the later reader may also have felt that their response was a rejoinder to the first annotator as well as to the author of the work; in a sense, this is a fragment of a historic conversation. Figure 4.18 is an example of someone annotating a book with one future reader directly in mind. The annotator was Hester Piozzi (1741–1821), also known as Hester Thrale after her first marriage, a close friend of the author Samuel Johnson (1709–1784) and a writer in her own right. In the closing years of her long life, Piozzi developed an intense friendship with a young man, Henry Conway, and regularly sent him gifts, including books that included her lengthy annotations. In these, she made a number of different interventions: critical guides to the text as well as historic references to the author (Johnson) and to her memories of him (Jackson, 2001, pp. 102–12). Her annotations can be set in the context of her well-known friendship and support of Johnson and of her own literary reputation.

Piozzi's marks of reading gain greater significance because they can be related back to a named individual and her known biographical circumstances; just as the anonymous readers of Figure 4.17 can be related back to the general circumstances of their time. The evidence for who owned and used any particular book is called provenance, and (once again seeing this in terms of the art market) this evidence can determine the economic value of a book.

This section has reviewed the major types of evidence that owners and readers have added to books: from their bookplates, signatures, reading notes and symbols, to handwriting practice. The variety of ways in which book users have left their marks testifies 'to the place of that book in the reader's social life, family history, professional practices, political commitments and devotional rituals', as William Sherman, scholar of the Renaissance, concludes from his survey of over 8000 early modern books (Sherman, 2008, p. iii).

Conclusion

This chapter has discussed the emergence of the printed book, from the late fifteenth-century luxury item to the small-format novel of the early nineteenth century. 'The form a given work appears in matters, and it signals participation in a series of aggregate changes to the concepts of reading, writing, and the book' (Runge, 2009, p. 15). Gutenberg's innovation in the production of movable metal type was taken up as a distinctive technology, and books rapidly stopped looking like manuscript copies. New features of printed books emerged in order to entice and guide readers, ranging from frontispieces to indexes. The availability of multiple versions of texts prompted new standards of comparison and critical commentary, leading to debates that are still current about the relationship between an author's intellectual creation, the text on the page, and its reception by readers. The fluid nature of the early centuries of book production has been compared here to the emergence of new ways of publishing via the web, involving similar issues of trust, intellectual property and instability of content.

Historic books set the challenge of linking the different conventions of early book production (which can be described and classified as part of an object life cycle) to the historic experiences of being a reader and user of books (the historic social contexts). Some of the snapshots offered in this chapter – such as Pepys choosing between binding styles, reproducing Shakespeare's portrait as a means of selling books, Piozzi writing her life into the margins of the books she gave to a young man – illuminate aspects of living with books that are uncommon in twenty-first-century experience. It has been possible to understand these physical aspects of books by putting them into their historical contexts.

This chapter has also explored ways in which the object life cycle needs to be supplemented by object biographies: an examination of the general production and uses of books does not describe the individual treatment that single books reveal. By the eighteenth century the level of experimentation in print was huge; innovations in print were a part of public discussion (Barchas, 2003, p. 6). This discussion included debate on the influence of increasingly cheap print on society; sometimes because the rapid proliferation of cheaper print was seen to be a bad thing, books were identified as contributing to a tidal wave of consumerism (Benedict, 2009, p. 287). These are familiar concerns in the present, except that today it is digital media (particularly social networking) that is the focus of discussion about identity, privacy, social mobility and behaviours.

References

Barchas, J. (2003) *Graphic Design, Print Culture and the Eighteenth-century Novel*, Cambridge, Cambridge University Press.

Benedict, B. (2009) 'Writing on writing: representations of the book in eighteenth-century literature', in Runge, L. and Rogers, P. (eds) *Producing the Eighteenth-century Book: Writers and Publishers in England, 1650–1800*, Newark, DE, University of Delaware Press, pp. 276–88.

Blayney, P. (1991) *The First Folio of Shakespeare*, Washington, DC, Folger Shakespeare Library.

Chartier, R. (1994 [1992]) *The Order of Books* (trans. from French by L. Cochrane), Stanford, CA, Stanford University Press.

Cooper, T. (2006) *Searching for Shakespeare*, London, National Portrait Gallery.

Feather, J. (2007) 'The British book market 1600–1800', in Eliot, S. and Rose, J. (eds) *A Companion to the History of the Book* [Online], Oxford, Blackwell. Available at http://www.blackwellreference.com/subscriber/tocnode?id=g9781405127653_chunk_g978140512765318 (Accessed 19 March 2014).

Genette, G. (1997 [1987]) *Paratexts: Thresholds of Interpretation* (trans. from French by J.E. Lewin), Cambridge, Cambridge University Press.

Gray, D. (2004 [2012]) 'Chaucer, Geoffrey (c.1340–1400)', in *Oxford Dictionary of National Biography* [Online], Oxford, Oxford University Press. Available at http://www.oxforddnb.com/view/article/5191 (Accessed 19 March 2014).]

Hellinga, L. (2007) 'The Gutenberg revolutions', in Eliot, S. and Rose, J. (eds) A *Companion to the History of the Book* [Online], Oxford, Blackwell. Available at http://www.blackwellreference.com/subscriber/tocnode?id=g9781405127653_chunk_g978140512765316 (Accessed 19 March 2014).

Internet World Stats, Usage and Population Statistics (2014) 'World Internet users and population statistics 2012' [Online]. Available at www.internetworldstats.com/stats.htm (Accessed 19 March 2014).

Jackson, H.J. (2001) *Marginalia: Readers Writing in Books*, New Haven, CN, and London, Yale University Press.

Nixon, H.M. (1984) *Catalogue of the Pepys Library at Magdalene College, Cambridge*, vol. 6: *Bindings*, Woodbridge/Totowa, NJ, DS Brewer/ Rowman and Littlefield.

Pearson, D. (2005) *English Bookbinding Styles 1450–1800*, London, British Library/Newcastle, DE, Oak Knoll Press.

Runge, L. (2009) 'Introduction', in Runge, L. and Rogers, P. (eds) *Producing the Eighteenth-century Book: Writers and Publishers in England, 1650–1800*, Newark, DE, University of Delaware Press, pp. 13–29.

Sherman, W. (2008) *Used Books: Marking Readers in Renaissance England*, Philadelphia, PA, University of Pennsylvania Press.

Tanselle, G.T. (1989) *A Rationale of Textual Criticism*, Philadelphia, PA, University of Pennsylvania Press.

UNESCO (2014) 'Memory of the world register' [Online]. Available at http://www.unesco.org/new/en/communication-and-information/ flagship-project-activities/memory-of-the-world/register/ (Accessed 19 March 2014).

Watson, R. (2007) 'Some non-textual uses of books', in Eliot, S. and Rose, J. (eds) *A Companion to the History of the Book* [Online], Oxford, Blackwell. Available at http://www.blackwellreference.com/subscriber/ book?id=g9781405127653_9781405127653 (Accessed 19 March 2014).

Further reading

David Pearson (2008) provides an extended discussion of the non-textual uses of books, championing the material qualities of historic books and explaining why we need to preserve the historic source material behind the unstoppable rise of digitisation projects. It is aimed at the general reader, as is Andrew Pettegree (2010), which discusses the economic, social and political contexts for books from Gutenberg to *c*.1600 in Europe. Topics include the impact of the Reformation, the rise of news pamphlets, censorship and second-hand books. Finally, Eleanor Shevlin (2010) has edited a reader, offering 25 reprinted texts that show how the study of eighteenth-century book history has developed over the last 60 years; it complements major narrative histories by presenting a range of voices and approaches.

Pearson, D. (2008) *Books as History: The Importance of Books Beyond Their Texts*, London, British Library.

Pettegree, A. (2010) *The Book in the Renaissance*, New Haven, CN, and London, Yale University Press.

Shevlin, E. (ed.) (2010) *The History of the Book in the West: 1700–1800*, Farnham, Ashgate.

Reading 4.1 Non-textual uses of books

Source: Watson, R. (2007) 'Some non-textual uses of books', in Eliot, S. and Rose, J. (eds) *A Companion to the History of the Book* **[Online], Oxford, Blackwell. Available at http://www. blackwellreference.com/subscriber/book? id=g9781405127653_9781405127653 (Accessed 19 March 2014).**

Anecdotes about the uses of books as physical objects abound. The literary historian knows that Samuel Johnson nearly brained the bookseller Thomas Osborne with a hefty tome during work on the catalogue of the Harleian collection (1743–5). Musicians know that John Cage's artwork, *Wild Edible Papers* (1990), made on the same principles as he composed his music, was his response to seeing the poor of Santiago, Chile, boiling books and newsprint to make the pulp edible. Anthropologists may be aware that a sage in Sub-Saharan Africa of the 1950s used a printed school book as part of equipment for divination. Students of Tibet learn that books were paraded unopened and used to line the tomb of a grand lama. What can stories such as these, and representations of books, tell us about the aura that surrounds books at any time? What are the messages of books when they appear in the visual iconography of any period?

[…]

'Associational copies': the book as relic

Relics – parts of a saint's body or objects used during their lifetime – were venerated by Christians from the fourth century. There was a lively trade in such things, since the presence of a famous relic could bring material as well as spiritual benefits to any church. Books used by saints were regarded as having special powers. When St. Patrick's tomb was opened in 553, some 60 years after his death according to the Annals of Ulster, his Gospel book was removed as a relic and bestowed on St. Columba. Books associated with saints Canice, Cronan, Declan, and Enda of Aran were similarly prized. Perhaps the best documented book of this kind is the Stonyhurst Gospel, written in Northumbria in the late seventh century in imitation of Italian books of the fifth to sixth centuries and removed from the tomb of St. Cuthbert (d.687) in 1104 (Brown 1969). John of Salisbury reported that Cuthbert had healed the sick by the laying-on of the book; St. Augustine had reported a similar practice to cure headaches. Other venerated books had similar powers:

a deluxe copy of St. Dionysius' works brought to St. Denis near Paris by legates of the Byzantine emperor in 827 performed nineteen miraculous cures the night it arrived. A copy of the *Cantigas de Santa Maria* (hymns to the Virgin) made for Alfonso X of Castile (1252–84) was placed on his chest to cure a threatening illness.

In Ireland, such works were frequently given metalwork cases to act as shrines. These shrines were used for activities as various as administering oaths, leading armies into battle, and the protection of tax gatherers. When the Normans defeated Domnall Ua Lochlainn in 1182, they took as spoil the Gospel of St. Martin, depriving the Irish of their special protection. The most celebrated book shrine is that of the Psalter of St. Colomba (521–97), known as the Cathach of Colmcille, made between 1062 and 1098 to the order of Cathbar O'Donnell. A sixteenth-century source records its function as a military trophy: carried to the right, three times around an army, it ensured victory. The power of manuscripts such as these had a long life: in 1627, the custodian of the Book of Durrow, then associated with St. Columba, was said to put water on the book and use it to cure sick cattle (Bede, d.735, had reported a similar practice with scrapings from Irish books to cure snake bites in his *Ecclesiastical History*). By the nineteenth century, books of this kind were sometimes the property of gentry families in Ireland, who hired them out for the taking of oaths (Lucas 1986).

Taking oaths upon the book

Medieval practice allowed a contract to be sworn in front of witnesses, upon relics or upon books. Even when recourse to properly constituted law courts was possible, details of legal transactions, especially the transfer of property to the Church, might be entered into a Gospel book or service book. The transaction was thus sanctioned by the full weight of religious authority. As late as c.1200, the administrators of St. Augustine's, Canterbury copied details of tenants, churches, and rents into a Gospel book. In late twelfth-century England, an oath taken upon a service book was challenged, it being held that kneeling before the Gospels was the correct procedure. This was certainly the case by the fifteenth century. Fear of divine retribution was a potent force against perjury.

Coronation oaths taken before the peers of the realm and parliament were not dependent upon any book, but the *Book of Oaths* of 1649 indicates that swearing 'by the holy contents of this book,' with a hand on the Bible, was usual practice by this date. Exceptions caused a stir. In 1657, Dr. Owen, Vice-Chancellor of Oxford, refused to be sworn as a witness by laying his right hand on the Bible and kissing it afterwards; legal opinion declared his oath invalid. When a Massachusetts colonist, Samuel Sewell, took the oath of allegiance in 1686, he held the book in his left hand, holding the right hand up to heaven, to the consternation of lawyers present. A German visitor seeking to use the Bodleian Library in 1710 was surprised to have to touch a Greek New Testament with his right hand and then kiss the book – an English postulant would perhaps have remarked only on the language of the sacred text (Spurr 2001). James Tyler's work on oaths of 1834 insisted that kissing the thumb and not the book made an oath invalid. William Congreve's play of 1700, *The Way of the World*, made use of this: when Mincing has to swear not to disclose what she has seen in the blue garret, she is clever enough to see that she is being asked to swear not on a Bible but on a book of poems. Kissing Bibles was deemed unhygienic by the end of the nineteenth century: on the advice of the medical profession, an act of 1909 discontinued the practice (Stringer 1910: 84).

Books that boast

It is easily said that individuals invested in books by way of illustration, ornament, or binding as a matter of prestige, as an aspiration, in order to establish themselves at an elevated point in a real or imagined social hierarchy. The theme is not always easy to document. Was investment in a beautifully illuminated Book of Hours a matter of social rivalry or a recognition that the cycle of prayer supported by such books, and the contact with the Almighty involved, deserved only the most expensive materials and workmanship? In the latter case, the embellishment was an act of piety, not display. There are certainly indications, however, that such books were intended to impress in public arenas. The fourteenth-century poet Eustache Deschamps (1346–1406) famously teased wealthy housewives of Paris for needing to appear in church with expensively decorated Books of Hours, and there are similar derogatory remarks about using prayer-books as a fashion accessory at later dates. Certainly, such books included more texts toward 1500 that were relevant for services in church rather than in private. When the covers of books used the same materials and ornament as contemporary fashions, we can assume that display was as significant as text. This was as true of the gorgeous textiles on the c.1400 binding of the Hours of the French queen, Isabel of Bavaria, as it was of the chaste black leather favored by ladies of Jansenist sympathies for similar books at Louis XIV's court.

The non-textual role of books such as these is underlined by the fact that they were kept not in libraries but as fashion accessories – as appears in the famous illuminated genealogy of the kings of Spain and Portugal by Simon Bening of 1530–34, where a Book of Hours appears in a box with rosaries and jewels as the accoutrements of a princess. From their appearance as independent texts in the thirteenth century, Books of Hours or similar devotional prayer-books became a standard sign of piety. The Virgin was commonly shown with such a book, and the clasping of books of this kind was the standard way of representing piety at a later date. In Protestant England, the descendants of Thomas More had themselves painted by Rowland Lockey in the late sixteenth century with such books in their hands as a sign of continued loyalty to the Church of Rome.

A Book of Hours is a Christian prayer-book, which, from the fourteenth century, was available in a small format for personal use.

Non-textual uses of libraries

Discussing the later Middle Ages, Armando Petrucci (1988) made a useful distinction between libraries that were intended for the distraction of their owners and those that were built up as an adjunct of power. The most prominent example of the latter was the library of Charles V of France (reigned 1364–80) who commissioned translations of authoritative texts of the medieval and classical past as a conscious policy to legitimate the new Valois dynasty. The works underpinned the ideology of royal government, one promoted by a corps of university-trained administrators. Many of these works have illustrated frontispieces that show the translator handing over the completed work to the king, placing the intellectual capital of the past under his protection.

As an attribute of state power, libraries such as this suffered the fortunes of the state in question. When Charles VIII of France conquered Naples in 1496, his opponent, King Alfonso II, took as much of the royal library as he could to the safety of Ischia. The French king was able to send over a thousand volumes back to France. Louis XII defeated the Sforza duke of Milan in 1499: almost half of the ducal library was removed from Pavia to the royal collection in Blois, the remainder being made available for the king's companions in arms. Both kings profited from the habit of Italian princes in developing libraries as acts of magnificence to broadcast their position as the heirs of ancient Rome. The memoirs of the Florentine bookseller Vespasiano da Bisticci make clear the role of libraries as instruments of prestige and conspicuous consumption for Renaissance potentates, even if we are less clear about the social rituals associated with them. We know that Borso d'Este paraded his magnificent Bible, illuminated by the most expensive illuminators of the land, as he journeyed to Rome in 1471 to receive the title of duke of Ferrara – this and a number of other works were given special luxury bindings and covers for the purpose.

Manifest signs of mastery of the intellectual and religious worlds encapsulated in books were necessary adjuncts for an effective display of power. Angelo Decembrio, the humanist servant of the future lord of Ferrara, described preparations for a reception given by his master in 1438 in the library of one of his courtiers: the aim was to upstage Florentine guests. The floor was strewn with cut flowers and the young prince gave a disquisition upon Terence and Donatus: the books were a setting that enabled the host to display literary refinement and total mastery of classical scholarship. The library of Federico da Motefeltro, lord of Urbino, in his palace at Gubbio had a similar role: from the 1470s it was open to the public, and the magnificently bound volumes were regularly shown to guests, ambassadors, and scholars, a crucial tool in the cultural politics and political maneuverings of its creator. Similar ambition was evidenced by François I when in August 1546 he treated English ambassadors to a discourse about his Greek books, bound in the new *alla greca* fashion from Italy, even though he knew none of the language.

The self-conscious development of libraries as physical expressions of their owner's relation to the intellectual capital of the day is something that has its own history. At what time does it become normal for the palaces of princes, the stately homes of aristocrats, and the manors of the gentry classes to include libraries that functioned on the same basis as other apartments? It is striking that Castiglione's *Book of the Courtier* first published in 1528 asks his courtier to be learned but almost to eschew contact with books. Sixteenth-century portraiture certainly confirms that courtiers, aristocrats, and gentlemen in general signified their social position by dress: books on the whole denoted those who needed them professionally, that is to say academics, clerics, or pedants. Henry Peachman's *Compleat Gentleman* (1622) likewise advises aspirant gentlemen not to be seen reading: learning was better developed by conversing with the learned. He refers to libraries amassed for show as a substitute for learning. Books that had too much gilding 'for ostentation sake,' he likened to 'prayer books of girls and gallants which are carried to the church but for their outsides.' However, he does recommend having those books that *were* owned by a gentleman properly bound and annotated by the owner to show that they had been studied.

Books and ornament

From the mid-fifteenth century, technological advances made decoration of run-of-the-mill books possible. Stamps, plaques, and rolls allowed covers to be decorated at little cost. From the 1470s, Italian binders imitated the Islamic practice of tooling gold onto leather, and this was taken up in northern Europe shortly before 1510. The design repertoire was largely peculiar to bindings, but the advent of strapwork and arabesque designs from the 1530s shows an effort to match ornament used for other articles: strapwork, in particular, could be found in the decoration of François I's Fontainebleau palace and on St. Porchaire ceramics, for example.

Any private library at this date was liable to be a collective resource, so that books needed to impress the friends of the owner. The French collector Jean Grolier had the words *Io. Grolierii et amicorum* impressed on his bindings; Willibald Pirkheimer (1470–1530) had a similar phrase on the bookplate Dürer designed for him. Books here appear as the physical manifestation of the cult of friendship and intellectual solidarity cultivated among humanistic scholars. Gabriel Naudé's 1627 publication about libraries assumed them to be accessible to a public beyond their owners. Lavish binding signaled that the object was worthy of respect and claimed homage from its users.

Books had always been used as gifts, though before the fifteenth century it is probably fair to say that the typical gift was from a potentate to the Church. By the Renaissance, scholars sought employment or favors by offering books to potential patrons. Deluxe books could be exchanged between rulers. Cosimo de' Medici had no qualms in sending, for example, a text of Livy corrected by Petrarch to the king of Naples in 1444. If in 1456 Francesco Sforza, duke of Milan, was advised that a horse might be a better present to the king of France than a book, later French kings were avid collectors of magnificent volumes.

In the nineteenth century, books were mass produced specifically to be offered as gifts. Companies like Alfred Mame in Tours and Martial Ardant in Limoges, from the 1850s, used the new-found ability of machines to block colorful designs onto cloth boards to create books intended as gifts at baptism, confirmation, and marriage, as well as school prizes and Christmas presents. Many surviving copies appear virtually unread. Similar books found a ready market in England, the covers broadcasting the taste and artistic culture of giver and recipient. John Ruskin was critical: of a gift book represented in Holman Hunt's *Awakening Conscience* (1854), he referred to 'embossed books, vain and useless, they also [like the furniture of the house] new, marked with no happy wearing of the beloved leaves.' Such books might be given singly or in sets. John Murray around 1848 marketed a set of small volumes of Byron's works in a miniature Grecian temple, covered in leather and with glass doors, which could hold its own with other ornaments on the mantelpiece (V&A, National Art Library, 802.AE.0042). In this period as much as in the fifteenth or sixteenth century, decoration gave a non-textual message; it showed investment in what the text represented (scholarship, religious orientation, literary refinement). Decorative binding was a corrective to the banality of the book as an object after the invention of printing.

[...]

The ultimate non-textual use of books is destruction. Today, people find it difficult to get rid of their books. Each represents a memory or act which may have little to do with the text. In the past, when books went out of fashion, they tended to be destroyed. In the first century of printing, university libraries throughout Europe jettisoned manuscript books as better printed editions became available.

Binders used leaves from discarded manuscript and printed books to strengthen bindings for some centuries. There are records of leaves from manuscript books being used to wrap up groceries and in the jakes in the sixteenth century (Brownrigg and Smith 2000: 22). Memory of this evidently lived on. In 1765, Thomas Gray, in his poem 'William Shakespeare to Mrs. Anne,' suggests that Mrs. Anne steal to a critic's closet to purloin his notes and use them as paper for baking and roasting.

Books have traditionally been burnt publicly as a gesture. Reformation Europe saw much of this as Protestants and Catholics sought to extinguish the memory of each other. The Index of the Catholic

Church, first instituted in 1559, drove many zealots to pitch forbidden books on the fire. This was the fate of the copy of Eric Cross's *The Tailor and Ansty* (1942) owned by the heroes of the story in rural Ireland. Once banned as obscene by the de Valera government on publication, three priests arrived at their house to throw their copy on the fire, even though, as Ansty remarked, it was worth eight shillings and sixpence. Some cities remind us of the consequences of burning books. From 1996, Bebelplatz in Berlin has had a memorial to Nazi burnings of books. The Judenplatz in Vienna from 1997 has had a work by Rachel Whiteread as a Holocaust Memorial, a cast of spaces around books on bookshelves, to signify books not written, not read, and not loved by citizens who were Jewish. Whether the symbolic role attributed to books will change as future generations rely on electronic means to store texts remains to be seen.

References and further reading

Brown, T. J. (ed.) (1969) *The Stonyhurst Gospel*. Oxford: Oxford University Press for the Roxburghe Club.

Brownrigg, L. L. and Smith, M. S. (eds.) (2000) *Interpreting and Collecting Fragments of Medieval Books*. Los Altos Hills: Anderson Lovelace.

Day, V. (2002) 'Portrait of a Provincial Artist: Jehan Gillemer, Poitevin Illuminator,' *Gesta*, (41) (1): 39–49.

Edwards, C. (2004) *Turning Houses into Homes*. Aldershot: Ashgate.

Kenyon, F. G. (1951) *Books and Readers in Ancient Greece and Rome*, 2nd edn. Oxford: Clarendon Press.

Leclercq, H. (1951) 'Sortes Sanctorum.' In *Dictionnaire d'archéologie chrétienne et de liturgie*, vol. 15, pt. 2, cols. 1590–2. Paris: Letouzey & Ané, 1907–53.

Lewis, B. (ed.) (1965) *Encyclopedia of Islam*, new edn., vol. II. Leiden: E. J. Brill.

Lucas, A. T. (1986) 'The Social Role of Relics and Reliquaries in Ancient Ireland,' *Journal of the Royal Society of Antiquaries of Ireland*, (116): 5–37.

Mayr-Harting, H. (1991) *Ottonian Book Illumination*, 2 vols. London: Harvey Miller.

Petrucci, A. (1988) 'Biblioteca di Corte e Cultura Libraria nella Napoli Aragonese.' In G. Cavallo (ed.), *Le biblioteche nel mondo antico e medievale*. Bari: Editori Laterza.

Spurr, J. (2001) 'A Profane History of Early Modern Oaths,' *Transactions of the Royal Historical Society*, 6th series, (11): 37–63.

Stringer, F. A. (1910) *Oaths and Affirmations*, 3rd edn. London: Stevens & Sons.

Thomas, K. (1971) *Religion and the Decline of Magic*, London: Weidenfeld and Nicolson.

Tye, L. (1998) *The Father of Spin: Edward L. Bernays and the Birth of Public Relations*. New York: Crown.

Afterword

This book has introduced you to some of the challenges for the academic study of material culture, and some of the solutions that have been developed since the nineteenth century, particularly within Anthropology and Archaeology. To remind you of how much the study of material culture has developed, think back to the materials you looked at in the 'Getting started' week. Here you worked with the earliest western museums: the private or semi-public collections assembled by scholars and merchants, known as cabinets of curiosities. These collections of intriguing natural and cultural objects, which might range from locally excavated prehistoric pots to stuffed crocodiles, could fill a glass case or a room in, to our eyes, no particular order. Cabinets of curiosity were increasingly popular by the 1600s: the same period that the printed book was becoming widely established and increasingly affordable – as discussed in Chapter 4. The collections and widely distributed books were both bearers of knowledge, on display for the viewer or reader.

This was the early modern period in Europe, when world views about what it was to be human were under pressure from new understandings of the place of the Earth in the solar system, and new challenges to the role of priests in the relationship between believers and the Christian God. Collections, whether of objects or of knowledge set out in books, were tools in the wider process of re-evaluating inherited beliefs and understandings in this period.

This book began by describing the author Petrarch, sitting in his Italian study with his books and ancient coins. He was at the beginning of the process of developing ways of testing and validating knowledge that resulted in the emergence of the scientific method still used today, which requires researchers to observe instead of repeating inherited wisdom. The use of movable type on a printing press, introduced a century after Petrarch lived, became a technology that made the comparison of versions of manuscript works much easier and gave rise to a foundation method of the humanities, critical practice, again based on close observation. Not taking objects for granted, and instead finding ways of looking closely and methodically at them, has had a transformative effect on western science and culture.

This is a very broad picture, and 'looking closely' has meant different things to different researchers over time. As you saw in Chapter 1, the study of humanity, past and present, has emerged out of massive inequalities in the distribution of power between anthropologists and the people they observed. While world politics today are very different from those during the period of western colonial expansion in the late nineteenth and early twentieth centuries, inequalities do remain but are now acknowledged as significant factors in conducting research. This self-awareness regarding the fact that research has an impact on its subjects has also become important inside museums, whose curators are now more aware of how cultural groups can be represented. Objects can represent people, and that is part of their enduring attraction, whether they stand in for a famous individual or provide a tangible connection to unknown hands that have held the same cooking pot, as you explored in Chapter 3. However, the academic study of material culture makes this apparently direct connection between object and owner a more complex relationship. There is, after Franz Boas, no 'natural' relationship between apparently similar objects distant in time and place from each other. It follows, as Chapter 2 explored, that there is no 'natural' way of describing an object, only multiple ways of creating a description: your selection of what is relevant to describe will depend on why you want to describe something.

We hope that you now have an emerging sense of how academic approaches to material culture differ from one another – an idea of how an anthropologist, for instance, might adopt a different approach from that of an art historian or an archaeologist. Later in the module you will be introduced to other disciplines which investigate material culture as well as texts, such as Religious Studies, History and Philosophy. As you will discover, academics working in these fields have different ideas about how objects should be studied, although they all give central importance to the skills of describing, contextualising and classifying which you have learned here. Grappling with such different ideas is part of the excitement and challenge of studying an interdisciplinary field such as material culture, which encourages you to recognise the multiplicity of approaches to objects, and to embrace all the new and different ways in which it is possible to make sense of them.

Glossary

atrium

In a Roman house, the first room after the entrance hall, usually a partly roofed space enabling rainwater to be collected in a pool in the centre of the room. Other rooms such as bedrooms would open from the atrium. The area was used for receiving visitors and for general family activities.

black-figure painting

A technique of vase painting in which figures and other decoration appear in black against a red background. This style flourished in Athens in the sixth century BCE. (See red-figure painting.)

bookplate

A small printed paper pasted into the front cover or title page of a book, showing the name of the owner (either a person or an institution), usually with a graphic design of heraldry or symbolic image relating to the owner.

codex

A book made up of folded parchment (prepared animal skin) or paper, stitched together along the fold: a form first used in the Roman empire in the first century CE.

collation

When used of manuscripts, this word signifies the process of comparison between different copies of the same or similar texts.

compositor

A specialist in a printing workshop who sets the pages of type.

context

The term used for all the surrounding objects, ideas or physical circumstances associated with an object.

copper plate

A technology of print reproduction, using a sheet of copper as the support for engraved lines. Ink trapped in the engravings was directly transferred to paper, using a press. The process was usually used for image reproduction, but occasionally for engraved text pages, too.

cultural evolution

The development of culture. During the late nineteenth and early twentieth centuries, it was widely held that cultures developed along a particular technological pathway, leading from barbarism to civilisation. We refer to this as the concept of 'unilinear cultural evolution'. Today, we no longer expect humans to adhere to any particular technological trajectory in their development through time, nor do we attach such strong moral and racial judgements to the technological achievements of different cultures.

cultural relativism

This is the principle that an individual's beliefs, practices and actions should be understood in terms of that individual's own culture.

emic

An emic description is one made from inside a culture. (See etic.)

ethnography

This can either mean the direct scientific study of particular human cultures, or it can refer more specifically to ways of writing about anthropological fieldwork based on participant observation.

etic

An etic description is one made from outside a culture. (See emic.)

evolutionary

This describes the gradual process by which something changes into a different form. Unilinear models of evolution assume a single pathway from simple to more complex forms.

exchange

The act of giving one thing and receiving another in return.

folio

As a specialist term for printed books, folio (from the Latin word for 'leaf') describes a full-sized sheet of paper folded once, creating two sheets, and also defines the size of the largest printed books. Paper folded twice creates four sheets, known as a quarto size.

font

In printing, the design of a complete set of letters, numbers, punctuation marks and other symbols.

frontispiece

The first image in a book, usually placed before the title page or incorporated into the title page.

gatherings

Groups of printed sheets folded in order, for sewing or glueing together into the codex form.

half-title

In a book, the page immediately before the title page, usually with an abbreviated form of the book title printed on it.

handmade

Constructed without the use of machines or tools. In the case of ceramic vessels, this means a vessel made from coiled clay rolls or slabs joined at their edges. It is also generally used to mean a ceramic object or part of an object not made using a potter's wheel.

handpress

The early printing press, operated by human muscle power.

inscription

Letters, words or phrases which are carved into, or painted on to, the surface of an object. Common inscriptions on Greek vases include the names of figures depicted on the vase, and the words *epoiesen* ('made by') and *egraphsen* ('painted by').

manicule

A symbol in the form of a pointing hand, drawn in the margin of a book by a reader to mark points of interest.

metadata

A set of data that describes and gives information about other data. For printed books, data such as the place of publication, the name of the font and the specification of the paper all describe aspects of the book production process relating to the book in which they are printed. A table of contents describes the structure of the work.

object-centred approach

An approach to the study of material culture that starts with a close description of the object and works outwards.

object-driven approach

An approach to the study of material culture that starts with the broader context in which objects are located and then works towards greater understanding of the object.

objective

A statement or observation independent of human existence or belief. It is the opposite of subjective.

octavo

As a specialist term for printed books, octavo (from the Latin word for 'eight') describes a full-sized sheet of paper folded four times, creating eight small sheets.

paratext

A term coined by the French literary theorist Gérard Genette as a specifically literary form of metadata. 'Para' is a prefix taken from the Greek word for 'from, by, besides, near'.

parchment

Animal skin (usually sheep or goat) prepared as a surface for ink, either handwritten or printed.

participant observation

Immersion in another society or social group for the purposes of understanding its ways of life.

peristyle

In a Roman house, a rectangular garden area surrounded by columns forming porticoes, usually on all four sides.

plainsong

A single, unaccompanied melodic line with a free rhythm delivered as a type of musical chanting in a religious context.

printing revolution

Historians' term for the rapid adoption of printing in Europe as a technology that supported social, political and economic shifts that can be seen to underpin the modern world.

provenance

The origin or source of something; the place where it is found. This term often also comes to stand in for the implications which derive from an object's presumed place of origin.

quarto

As a specialist term for printed books, quarto (from the Latin word for 'four') describes a full-sized sheet of paper folded twice, creating four small sheets.

reciprocity

The informal systems of exchange of goods and services associated with non-market economies. It is often used as a way of describing the delayed return of goods or services built up through obligation of various kinds.

red-figure painting

A technique of vase painting in which figures and other decoration appear in red (the natural colour of the fired clay) against a black background. This style was probably developed in Athens around 530 BCE. (See black-figure painting.)

slip

A liquid mixture of clay and water, often used for decorating pottery, or for joining together the different parts of a clay vessel.

subjective

A statement or opinion that is not independent of human existence or consciousness. It is the opposite of objective.

vellum

Finest quality parchment, made from young animals (lamb, kid or calf).

wheel-turned

Used to describe a ceramic vessel made using a potter's wheel.

white-ground painting

A technique of vase painting in which a white clay slip is applied to the surface of a vase. This white background can then be painted using other colours, such as yellow, pink, red, violet and blue. This style flourished in Athens during the fifth century BCE.

Acknowledgements

Chapter 2

Reynolds. N. (2005) 'Royal heirlooms for sale to pay death duties', *The Daily Telegraph*, 14 November. Daily Telegraph, Telegraph Media Group Ltd, London.

Chapter 3

Radice, B. (trans. with introduction) (1969 [1963]) *The Letters of the Younger Pliny*, Harmondsworth, Penguin Classics. Copyright © Betty Radice 1963, 1969.

Chapter 4

Watson, R. (2007) 'Some non-textual uses of books', in Eliot, S. and Rose, J. (eds) *A Companion to the History of the Book*, Chichester, Blackwell Publishing Ltd. Reproduced with permission of Blackwell Publishing Ltd.

Every effort has been made to contact copyright holders. If any have inadvertently been overlooked the publishers will be pleased to make the necessary arrangements at the first opportunity.

Index